Introduction

- Setting the stage for advanced Illustrator usage

- Importance of mastering advanced techniques

Chapter 1: Beyond the Basics

- Recap of essential Illustrator tools and functions

- Transitioning from beginner to advanced user mindset

- Emphasizing the need for efficiency and creativity

Chapter 2: Mastering Advanced Tools

- In-depth exploration of advanced drawing and shaping tools

- Creative use of the Pen Tool, Curvature Tool, and Anchor Point manipulation

- Demonstrating the power of the Shape Builder Tool

Chapter 3: Vector Artistry Unleashed

- Understanding vector graphics and their advantages

- Advanced techniques for creating intricate vector artwork

- Leveraging gradients, patterns, and blends to add depth

Chapter 4: Precision Typography
- Exploring advanced typography tools and techniques

- Creating custom type designs and layouts

- Working with text on paths and within shapes

Chapter 5: Advanced Blending and Masking
- Harnessing the potential of blending modes and opacity settings

- Mastering complex masking techniques for creative effects

- Creating seamless compositions using Clipping Masks and Opacity Masks

Chapter 6: 3D Effects and Perspective
- Introducing Illustrator's 3D capabilities for dynamic designs

- Creating 3D objects, text, and effects

- Implementing perspective grids for realistic depth

Chapter 7: Advanced Color and Gradient Techniques
- Delving into color theory and its application in Illustrator

- Creating and using custom color swatches and libraries

- Blending and meshing gradients for captivating visual effects

Chapter 8: Artboards and Advanced Layouts
- Maximizing efficiency with multiple artboards

- Creating presentations, mockups, and multi-page documents

- Techniques for responsive and adaptive design using artboards

Chapter 9: Data Visualization and Infographics
- Designing compelling data visualizations with charts and graphs

- Crafting informative infographics using advanced layout techniques

- Incorporating interactivity for digital publications

Chapter 10: Automation and Workflow Enhancements

- Streamlining repetitive tasks with Actions and Batch Processing

- Utilizing scripts and plug-ins for extended functionality

- Integrating Illustrator with other Adobe Creative Cloud applications

Chapter 11: Exporting and Collaboration

- Choosing the right file formats for different purposes

- Preparing designs for print, web, and mobile

- Collaborative workflows using cloud-based services and shared libraries

Conclusion

- Recap of key takeaways from the book

- Encouragement to continue exploring and pushing the boundaries

- Final thoughts on achieving brilliance in Illustrator's advanced usage

Appendix:

- Resources for further learning and exploration

- Glossary of advanced Illustrator terminology

INTRODUCTION
SETTING THE STAGE FOR ADVANCED ILLUSTRATOR USAGE

Adobe Illustrator stands as a veritable playground for creative minds, offering a rich array of tools and functions to bring ideas to life in stunning visual form. If you've been navigating the realm of vector design, you're likely familiar with the basics—shapes, lines, and colors. But now, it's time to embark on a journey that will elevate your Illustrator prowess to new heights. Welcome to the world of advanced usage, where your creations will radiate brilliance and sophistication.

Why Master Advanced Techniques?
Before we dive into the intricacies of Illustrator's advanced capabilities, let's pause for a moment to consider why venturing into this territory is worth the effort. While mastering the basics equips you with the foundation to create, advancing into more complex techniques enables you to craft designs that are not only visually appealing but also captivating, innovative, and unforgettable.

Advanced Illustrator techniques open doors to endless possibilities. Imagine effortlessly manipulating anchor points to shape intricate designs, using gradients to add depth and dimension, seamlessly blending colors to create realistic textures, and crafting 3D effects that give your artwork a sense of realism. These techniques provide you with the tools to evoke emotions, tell stories, and communicate ideas with exceptional clarity.

Transitioning from Basics to Brilliance
Shifting from basic to advanced usage in Illustrator requires a shift in mindset. It's not just about knowing where the tools are located or what they do; it's about understanding how to use them creatively and efficiently to achieve your desired outcomes. It's about discovering the hidden potential within each tool and function.

As you embark on this journey, embrace a sense of curiosity and experimentation. Approach each tool as if it were an instrument in an orchestra, waiting to harmonize with others to create a symphony of design. Recognize that mistakes are stepping stones to mastery. Push your boundaries, challenge your comfort zones, and explore the uncharted territories of your creativity.

Efficiency and Creativity: The Dynamic Duo
The hallmark of advanced Illustrator users lies in their ability to balance efficiency and creativity. While it's true that Illustrator offers a plethora of tools, palettes, and options, advanced users know when to wield them with precision and finesse. Rather than overwhelming themselves with every available feature, they choose the ones that align with their

creative vision, using them effectively to produce exceptional results.

Efficiency is not just about speed; it's about working smarter. Advanced users develop workflows that minimize redundant tasks and maximize the time spent on creative decision-making. They understand that a well-organized workspace, the use of shortcuts, and the mastery of key commands contribute to a seamless design process.

Creativity, on the other hand, thrives when boundaries are pushed and conventions are challenged. By delving into advanced techniques, you'll be able to breathe life into your ideas like never before. Whether it's crafting intricate typography, designing immersive 3D scenes, or creating data-driven visualizations, these techniques enable you to explore the outer reaches of your imagination.

The Journey Ahead
In the chapters that follow, we will embark on a comprehensive exploration of Illustrator's advanced capabilities. We will delve into the nuances of vector artistry, typography, blending and masking, color manipulation, 3D effects, advanced layouts, and even automation. Each chapter will be a gateway to unveiling the true brilliance that Illustrator can offer.

Remember, the path to mastery is a continuous one. As you absorb the knowledge within these pages, practice is key. Take the time to experiment with each technique, apply it to your projects, and adapt it to your unique style. Let the knowledge you gain become a part of your creative DNA, allowing you to create designs that not only catch the eye but also captivate the soul.

So, buckle up and get ready to embark on a transformative journey. Illustrator Brilliance awaits, and you're about to unlock the door to a world where your creativity knows no bounds. Get ready to shine!

IMPORTANCE OF MASTERING ADVANCED TECHNIQUES

In the vast realm of digital design, proficiency with basic tools can only take you so far. To truly harness the full potential of your creativity and stand out as a design virtuoso, delving into the realm of advanced techniques is not just an option—it's a necessity. This article delves into the significance of mastering advanced techniques in Adobe Illustrator and how they can reshape your design journey.

Elevating Your Creative Expression
At the heart of mastering advanced techniques lies the ability to elevate your creative expression to new heights. While basic skills enable you to create functional designs, advanced techniques empower you to infuse your work with personality, emotion, and a distinctive style. It's like upgrading from a simple

pencil sketch to a breathtaking oil painting—your designs become more vibrant, nuanced, and captivating.

Imagine manipulating vector paths with surgical precision, effortlessly crafting intricate patterns that mesmerize the viewer, or using advanced typography techniques to transform text into a work of art. These capabilities give you the power to breathe life into your ideas and create designs that resonate deeply with your audience.

Setting Yourself Apart in a Crowded Space
In today's digital age, the competition in the design landscape is fierce. Clients and audiences are inundated with an array of visual content vying for their attention. So, how do you rise above the noise? The answer lies in your ability to offer something exceptional, something that stands out in a sea of mediocrity.

Mastery of advanced Illustrator techniques provides you with a unique edge. It enables you to produce designs that are not only visually stunning but also conceptually groundbreaking. Whether it's through innovative use of gradients, masterful blending modes, or the creation of intricate vector art, your designs will command attention and leave a lasting impression.

Unleashing Your Imagination

One of the most exciting aspects of mastering advanced techniques is the newfound freedom it grants your imagination. Think of Illustrator as a vast playground of creative possibilities, and these advanced techniques are the keys that unlock its hidden treasures.

Want to design a surreal landscape that seamlessly merges reality and fantasy? Advanced blending and masking techniques make it possible. Dreaming of turning your typography into a dynamic visual experience? Advanced type manipulation tools can make it a reality. The more you master these techniques, the more you liberate your imagination from the confines of the ordinary.

Broadening Your Design Repertoire

Design is a dynamic field that demands versatility. While basic design skills can help you tackle straightforward projects, they may fall short when faced with more complex and innovative challenges. Mastering advanced techniques equips you with an expansive toolkit to tackle a wider range of projects.

From crafting intricate logos to designing captivating infographics, advanced Illustrator techniques enable you to adapt to various design briefs with finesse. This adaptability not only opens doors to new opportunities but also ensures that your skills remain relevant in an ever-evolving design landscape.

Fueling Continuous Growth

The journey of mastering advanced techniques is not a destination; it's an ongoing adventure. Each new technique you learn, each creative breakthrough you achieve, fuels your growth as a designer. It challenges you to push boundaries, refine your skills, and explore uncharted territories.

As you delve deeper into the world of advanced techniques, you'll discover that the more you learn, the more you realize there's still more to explore. This perpetual cycle of learning and growth keeps your passion for design alive and ensures that you remain at the forefront of your craft.

In Conclusion

Mastering advanced techniques in Adobe Illustrator is not just about acquiring technical skills; it's about transforming your design journey. It's about transcending the ordinary, capturing attention, and expressing your creativity in ways you never thought possible. With each technique you master, you'll be one step closer to creating designs that leave a lasting imprint on hearts and minds. So, embrace the challenge, embark on the journey, and let the brilliance of advanced techniques illuminate your design path.

CHAPTER 1: BEYOND THE BASICS
RECAP OF ESSENTIAL ILLUSTRATOR TOOLS AND FUNCTIONS

Adobe Illustrator, the venerable software in the realm of digital design, serves as both a canvas and a toolkit for artists, illustrators, and designers. From precise vector drawings to intricate typographic compositions, Illustrator's capabilities are as diverse as the imagination itself. In this article, we'll embark on a comprehensive recap of the essential Illustrator tools and functions, laying a strong foundation for your creative journey.

1. Selection Tools: Your Starting Point
At the heart of any design project lies the ability to select, move, and manipulate elements. Illustrator's selection tools are your virtual hands, enabling you to choose and transform objects with finesse. From the simple Selection Tool to the powerful Direct Selection Tool, these tools provide the basic building blocks for your design process.

2. Pen Tool: Precision Personified
The Pen Tool is the hallmark of vector design. Its ability to create and edit paths with precise anchor points lays the groundwork for intricate shapes and forms. While it can be intimidating at first, mastery of the Pen Tool allows you to achieve fluid curves, sharp angles, and complex shapes that define vector art.

3. Shape Tools: Foundational Elements

Illustrator's Shape Tools—Rectangle, Ellipse, Polygon, and more—offer a straightforward way to create basic geometric forms. These tools are ideal for laying the groundwork of your designs before delving into more intricate details.

4. Type Tools: Text with Style

Typography is a cornerstone of design, and Illustrator's Type Tools provide a variety of options for manipulating text. From the simple Type Tool for basic text input to the Type on a Path Tool for wrapping text around shapes, these tools let you create expressive and visually engaging typography.

5. Pen and Pencil Brushes: Stroke of Creativity

The Brush Tools—Pen and Pencil—let you draw freehand strokes and paths. With the Pencil Brush, you can achieve the organic feel of hand-drawn sketches, while the Pen Brush offers the precision of vector lines. These tools give life to your illustrations, enabling you to infuse your designs with your unique style.

6. Gradient and Color Tools: Shades of Expression

Colors breathe life into designs, and Illustrator's Gradient and Color Tools allow you to explore a spectrum of hues, shades, and tones. From simple solid colors to complex gradients, these tools help you evoke emotions and set the mood of your creations.

7. Pathfinder: Shaping New Realities

The Pathfinder panel is a hidden gem for creating complex shapes through the combination and subtraction of simpler forms. Uniting, dividing, and intersecting shapes, this tool empowers you to craft intricate designs that transcend the limitations of basic shapes.

8. Layers and Groups: Organizational Magic

A cluttered workspace can stifle creativity, which is where Layers and Groups come to the rescue. These organizational tools help you manage complex projects by separating elements, making editing more convenient, and preserving your design's hierarchy.

9. Transform Tools: Shape-Shifting Wonders

Scaling, rotating, reflecting, and shearing—these Transform Tools enable you to reshape your elements effortlessly. They give you the power to manipulate objects in ways that fit your creative vision, making them crucial for achieving a harmonious composition.

10. Artboards: Canvas Expansion

Artboards are your creative canvases within Illustrator. They allow you to work on multiple designs within a single document, helping you create variations, prototypes, or even multi-page projects all in one place.

In Conclusion

These essential Illustrator tools and functions lay the groundwork for your creative journey. Mastery of these basics provides you with a solid foundation to experiment, explore, and ultimately excel in the world of vector design. As you become familiar with these tools, you'll be well-prepared to venture into the more advanced techniques that Illustrator has to offer, propelling your designs to new heights of creativity and innovation. So, embrace these tools, experiment, and watch your creative vision come to life with Adobe Illustrator.

TRANSITIONING FROM BEGINNER TO ADVANCED USER MINDSET

Stepping into the world of Adobe Illustrator is like entering a realm of limitless creative possibilities. From your first encounter with basic shapes to your journey into intricate vector art, you've come a long way. Now, as you stand at the threshold of advanced Illustrator usage, it's time to make a significant shift in mindset. In this article, we'll explore the journey of transitioning from a beginner to an advanced user mindset in Adobe Illustrator, unlocking the doors to unparalleled design brilliance.

Embracing the Growth Mindset

At the heart of the transition lies a shift in mindset—an evolution from a fixed mindset to a growth mindset. A fixed mindset views skills and abilities as innate traits, while a growth mindset sees them as qualities that can be developed through effort, practice, and learning.

As you transition from a beginner to an advanced user, adopting a growth mindset is paramount. Embrace challenges, view mistakes as learning opportunities, and understand that your skills are not fixed but rather fluid and expandable. This mindset shift is the foundation upon which advanced mastery is built.

Exploring Curiosity and Experimentation

Beginners often approach Illustrator with caution, sticking to what they know works. Advanced users, however, thrive on curiosity and experimentation. They're not afraid to venture into uncharted territories, test new techniques, and explore unfamiliar tools. This willingness to experiment is where true creativity flourishes.

Give yourself permission to play, to create without predefined expectations. Push the boundaries of what you think is possible, and don't be deterred by initial failures. Each experiment, successful or not, contributes to your growth as a designer.

Mastering Efficiency and Workflow

Transitioning to an advanced user mindset involves a shift from focusing solely on the tools to optimizing your workflow. Advanced users understand that time is a valuable resource, and efficiency is the key to unlocking more creative time.

Learn keyboard shortcuts, organize your workspace, and develop systematic workflows that streamline your design process. Efficient use of tools not only enhances your productivity but also frees your mind to focus on the creative decisions that truly matter.

Cultivating Attention to Detail
While beginners are often focused on achieving basic functionality, advanced users dive deep into the nuances of design. They pay attention to the tiniest details that contribute to the overall aesthetics and impact of their work.
Zoom in, scrutinize anchor points, adjust gradients, and fine-tune typography. These details might seem minor, but they collectively elevate your design from good to exceptional. It's the difference between a design that merely works and one that resonates profoundly.

Learning the Art of Iteration
The path to mastery is paved with iteration. Advanced users understand that their initial designs are rarely their best. They embrace a continuous cycle of creation, evaluation, and refinement.
Don't be discouraged if your first attempt doesn't meet your expectations. Instead, iterate, refine, and improve. Each iteration brings you closer to your

creative vision, helping you uncover the hidden gems that lie beneath the surface.

Collaborating and Seeking Feedback
Advanced users recognize the value of collaboration and feedback. They understand that fresh perspectives can shed light on blind spots and offer insights that propel their designs forward.

Seek feedback from peers, mentors, or online communities. Constructive criticism helps you view your work from different angles, sparking new ideas and refining your designs. Collaborative efforts not only enhance your skills but also expand your creative horizons.

In Conclusion
Transitioning from a beginner to an advanced user mindset in Adobe Illustrator is a transformative journey. It's not just about mastering tools; it's about embracing a mindset that thrives on curiosity, experimentation, and continuous growth. As you navigate this evolution, remember that advanced mastery is a culmination of mindset, skill, and creative expression. Embrace challenges, welcome exploration, and let your journey from novice to virtuoso in Adobe Illustrator be a testament to the limitless possibilities of the human imagination.

EMPHASIZING THE NEED FOR EFFICIENCY AND CREATIVITY

In the dynamic realm of design, efficiency and creativity stand as two sides of the same coin. Just as a symphony requires both melody and rhythm, successful design endeavors necessitate a seamless blend of these two essential elements. In this article, we delve into the symbiotic relationship between efficiency and creativity, highlighting why their harmonious integration is the key to unlocking your true design potential.

Efficiency: The Backbone of Productivity

Efficiency is not about cutting corners or sacrificing quality—it's about optimizing your workflow to achieve more in less time. In the realm of design, where deadlines loom and client expectations run high, efficiency is the linchpin that allows you to meet demands without compromising on creativity.

1. Streamlined Workflows for Uninterrupted Creativity

Efficiency empowers you to work smarter, not harder. By mastering keyboard shortcuts, customizing your workspace, and utilizing presets, you can navigate Illustrator with finesse. These shortcuts save precious seconds that add up over the course of a project, leaving you with more time to focus on the creative aspects of your design.

2. Templates and Libraries: Accelerating Design Creation

Templates and libraries serve as your creative arsenal, allowing you to reuse and adapt existing assets. Whether it's a customized color palette, a logo template, or a library of vector elements, these resources streamline your design process, providing a strong foundation on which creativity can flourish.

3. Consistency and Branding: Efficient Design Language

Efficiency also extends to maintaining visual consistency across projects. Establishing a clear design language and adhering to brand guidelines not only streamlines your decision-making but also reinforces your client's brand identity. This consistency is achieved efficiently through the application of established design principles.

Creativity: The Spark of Innovation

While efficiency paves the way, creativity provides the spark that ignites innovation. Creativity is not just about producing novel designs; it's about crafting solutions that engage, resonate, and leave a lasting impact.

1. Creative Problem-Solving for Unique Solutions

Creativity thrives when you approach problems with an open mind. It encourages you to explore unorthodox angles, envision multiple solutions, and find the one that aligns with your artistic vision. The ability to think outside the box and apply creative problem-solving is what distinguishes mundane designs from exceptional ones.

2. Innovation and Originality: Pushing Boundaries

Efficiency may help you produce designs swiftly, but it's creativity that makes your work stand out. Experiment with new techniques, challenge conventional norms, and dare to push the boundaries of design. It's through this exploration that you unearth fresh perspectives and innovative approaches that captivate your audience.

3. Emotional Resonance and Storytelling

Effective design is not solely about aesthetics; it's about conveying emotions and telling stories. Creativity allows you to infuse your designs with narratives that evoke feelings and forge connections. Whether it's through color choices, typography, or imagery, your creative decisions shape the narrative your design communicates.

The Dance of Efficiency and Creativity

The synergy between efficiency and creativity is akin to a dance—an intricate choreography that blends practicality with artistic flair. Balancing these two elements requires finesse, as neither should overpower the other. An overemphasis on efficiency might lead to sterile designs lacking emotional resonance, while an exclusive focus on creativity could result in missed deadlines and chaotic workflows.

The true magic lies in striking a harmonious equilibrium. As you create, keep an eye on efficiency to ensure your process remains smooth and productive. Simultaneously, let creativity flow freely, enriching your designs with innovative concepts, unexpected twists, and imaginative brilliance.

In Conclusion
Efficiency and creativity are not opposing forces; they are allies that, when harnessed together, amplify your design prowess. A workflow streamlined for efficiency liberates your mind to explore the depths of creative expression. In the end, it's the harmonious marriage of these two forces that transforms your designs from mere visuals into captivating narratives that leave a lasting imprint on hearts and minds. So, let efficiency and creativity guide your steps as you navigate the intricate dance of design.

CHAPTER 2: MASTERING ADVANCED TOOLS
IN-DEPTH EXPLORATION OF ADVANCED DRAWING
AND SHAPING TOOLS

In the realm of digital design, Adobe Illustrator stands as an unparalleled canvas where imagination comes to life through vector artistry. While mastering the basics of drawing and shaping lays the foundation, delving into advanced techniques catapults your designs into a realm of complexity and creativity. In this article, we embark on an in-depth exploration of the advanced drawing and shaping tools within Illustrator, unraveling the secrets to creating intricate and captivating vector artworks.

The Power of Advanced Drawing Tools

Advanced drawing tools in Illustrator offer a playground of possibilities for crafting intricate shapes, unique compositions, and captivating visuals. Beyond the basic Pen and Shape Tools, these advanced tools provide the key to unlocking your creative potential.

1. Curvature Tool: Fluidity in Design

The Curvature Tool introduces a sense of fluidity to your vector drawings. With the ability to create and adjust curves effortlessly, it allows for the creation of intricate, organic shapes that are challenging to achieve using traditional tools. Whether it's flowing lines or complex paths, the Curvature Tool grants you the freedom to shape your ideas with grace.

2. Width Tool: Adding Dimension to Strokes

The Width Tool lets you manipulate the thickness of stroke paths, creating dynamic and visually appealing designs. By varying the width along the length of a stroke, you can mimic the effect of pressure-sensitive brushes and give your designs a hand-drawn touch.

3. Blob Brush Tool: Painterly Precision

The Blob Brush Tool bridges the gap between vector and traditional painting. It enables you to create shapes with a brush-like stroke, providing a painterly quality that adds depth and character to your illustrations. This tool is particularly valuable when crafting organic and expressive forms.

4. Perspective Grid: Dimensionality and Realism

The Perspective Grid tool catapults your designs into a three-dimensional space. It's an indispensable tool when creating scenes with depth, such as architectural illustrations, product mockups, or landscapes. The Perspective Grid ensures that objects align with vanishing points, resulting in a more realistic and immersive visual experience.

Mastering Shaping Techniques

Shaping in Illustrator involves not just the creation of basic forms but also the transformation and manipulation of shapes to create complex designs. Advanced shaping techniques offer precision and finesse, enabling you to craft intricate designs with ease.

1. Shape Builder Tool: Merging and Dividing
The Shape Builder Tool is a game-changer for creating complex shapes from basic forms. It allows you to merge and subtract shapes intuitively, providing a dynamic way to experiment with compositions. This tool encourages experimentation, enabling you to visualize and refine design concepts seamlessly.

2. Pathfinder Panel: The Magic of Compound Shapes
The Pathfinder Panel is a treasure trove of tools for creating compound shapes through operations like unite, intersect, exclude, and more. These tools let you create intricate designs by combining, subtracting, or dividing shapes. The Pathfinder Panel is particularly valuable for logo design, icon creation, and abstract artwork.

3. Envelope Distort: Warp and Bend
The Envelope Distort tools provide the ability to warp, bend, and manipulate objects within custom shapes. Whether you're designing label graphics that conform to a curved surface or creating text that follows the contours of an object, these tools offer flexibility and creative possibilities.

4. Blend Tool: Seamless Transitions
The Blend Tool allows you to create smooth transitions between shapes, colors, and sizes. It's a fantastic tool for creating gradients that merge seamlessly, giving your designs a cohesive and visually

appealing appearance. This tool is especially useful for creating abstract art and patterns.

Embracing Creativity through Advanced Drawing and Shaping

As you delve into the depths of advanced drawing and shaping tools within Illustrator, you're embarking on a journey of unbridled creativity. The blend of precision, finesse, and imagination enables you to create designs that transcend the ordinary and enter the realm of the extraordinary.

Through the Curvature Tool, you'll craft fluid forms that evoke movement. The Width Tool allows you to play with dimensionality, while the Blob Brush Tool grants your designs a painterly touch. The Perspective Grid breathes life into three-dimensional scenes, and the Shape Builder Tool empowers you to merge and divide shapes intuitively.

With the Pathfinder Panel, you'll discover the magic of compound shapes, while the Envelope Distort tools let you warp and bend with precision. Finally, the Blend Tool facilitates seamless transitions, weaving patterns and gradients with elegance.

In Conclusion

Advanced drawing and shaping tools in Adobe Illustrator are your keys to unlocking a world of limitless creativity. By mastering these tools, you empower yourself to craft designs that blend precision and imagination seamlessly. These tools are not just features; they are the brushes and chisels of the digital artist, enabling you to mold and sculpt your ideas into breathtaking works of art. Embrace the complexity, experiment with finesse, and let your designs flourish as you harness the full potential of advanced drawing and shaping in Adobe Illustrator.

CREATIVE USE OF THE PEN TOOL, CURVATURE TOOL, AND ANCHOR POINT MANIPULATION

In the realm of vector design, few tools hold as much significance as the Pen Tool, Curvature Tool, and the intricate world of anchor point manipulation. These tools are the sculptor's chisel, the artist's brush strokes, and the architect's blueprint—all rolled into one. In this article, we embark on a creative journey through the mastery of the Pen Tool, Curvature Tool, and the art of manipulating anchor points in Adobe Illustrator, discovering how these tools can transform your visions into intricate digital masterpieces.

The Pen Tool: Precision and Prowess
The Pen Tool is both an ally and a challenge—an indispensable instrument that separates the novices from the virtuosos. At its core, the Pen Tool empowers you to create complex, precise shapes and paths with unparalleled control.

1. The Art of Curves and Anchors

To truly harness the creative potential of the Pen Tool, understand the interplay between curves and anchors. Click to create anchor points and drag to adjust the handles that define the curvature. Learning to manipulate these handles with finesse grants you mastery over graceful curves and sharp angles.

2. From Paths to Shapes

The Pen Tool doesn't just create paths; it transforms them into shapes. By closing a path, you create a shape that can be filled, stroked, or manipulated further. This transition from paths to shapes unlocks an entire world of possibilities—from intricate logos to detailed illustrations.

3. Bezier Mastery

Bezier curves are the foundation of vector artistry. The Pen Tool's handles allow you to control the direction and curvature of each curve segment. By understanding the delicate dance between anchor points and handles, you gain the ability to mold your designs with precision.

Curvature Tool: Flowing Elegance

The Curvature Tool enters the scene as a more intuitive counterpart to the Pen Tool. It's the artist's brush, allowing you to sketch fluid lines and shapes with natural hand movements.

1. Fluidity of Curves
The Curvature Tool lets you create and edit paths with a sense of flow. Click to add points, and click-drag to create curves. This fluidity is particularly valuable when crafting organic shapes, such as natural forms or free-flowing designs.

2. Simplicity and Intuitiveness
While the Pen Tool requires careful consideration of anchor points and handles, the Curvature Tool offers a more intuitive approach. It's a fantastic tool for those who prioritize the creative process over technical intricacies.

3. The Curvature of Anchors
Similar to the Pen Tool, the Curvature Tool's magic lies in anchor points. By clicking and dragging anchor points, you can fine-tune the curvature of your lines and shapes, creating designs that effortlessly guide the viewer's eye.

Anchor Point Manipulation: Sculpting Precision
Manipulating anchor points is akin to sculpting clay—each tweak and adjustment shapes your design with precision. Whether you're using the Pen Tool or the Curvature Tool, understanding anchor point manipulation is essential for creating intricate designs.

1. Direct Selection and Path Modification

The Direct Selection Tool is your go-to for anchor point manipulation. Clicking an anchor point with this tool allows you to adjust its position or handles individually. By selecting and shifting anchor points, you can refine the contours of your shapes.

2. Bezier Handles and Control

Fine-tuning anchor points involves manipulating their handles. To create sharp angles, pull handles close to the anchor point; for smooth curves, extend handles outward. This level of control grants you the ability to sculpt paths to your exact specifications.

3. The Anchor Point Tool: Adding and Deleting Anchors

The Anchor Point Tool provides even more precision by allowing you to add and delete anchor points. This tool is invaluable when refining existing paths, eliminating unnecessary points, and maintaining a clean and efficient design structure.

Unlocking Creative Expression

Mastery of the Pen Tool, Curvature Tool, and anchor point manipulation is more than technical prowess; it's a journey toward creative freedom. These tools are your instruments for translating concepts into tangible designs, for infusing your creations with personality and precision.

Through the Pen Tool's curves and anchors, you craft intricate forms. The Curvature Tool offers the freedom of natural sketching, while anchor point manipulation empowers you to sculpt precision. Every line you draw, every anchor you adjust, contributes to a symphony of creativity and design.

In Conclusion

The Pen Tool, Curvature Tool, and anchor point manipulation are your brushes, your chisels, your tools of creation in Adobe Illustrator. They allow you to breathe life into your ideas, to mold paths and shapes that express your unique vision. As you dive into the intricacies of these tools, remember that the true artistry lies not just in their technical mastery but in the stories they help you tell through your designs. Embrace the curves, cherish the anchors, and let your creativity flow through every path you shape in the digital realm.

DEMONSTRATING THE POWER OF THE SHAPE BUILDER TOOL

In the world of vector design, precision and innovation are paramount. Every path, every shape, and every composition is a testament to the designer's skill and imagination. Amidst the array of tools at your disposal, the Shape Builder Tool in Adobe Illustrator stands out as a dynamic force that empowers you to transcend traditional boundaries and craft designs that are both intricate and captivating. In this article, we embark on a journey to demonstrate the immense power of the Shape Builder Tool, showcasing how it can revolutionize your creative process and elevate your designs to new heights.

The Essence of the Shape Builder Tool

At its core, the Shape Builder Tool is a bridge between creativity and efficiency. It transcends the limitations of traditional shape creation and manipulation, providing a dynamic and intuitive approach to design. This tool allows you to merge, divide, and transform shapes in a way that encourages experimentation and unlocks unexpected outcomes.

1. Merging and Creating Complex Forms

One of the most remarkable features of the Shape Builder Tool is its ability to merge multiple shapes into complex forms with a simple drag-and-release motion. By selecting multiple overlapping shapes and dragging across them, you seamlessly combine them into unified compositions.

Imagine the creation of intricate logos, abstract patterns, or stylized illustrations. The Shape Builder Tool makes the process swift and organic, allowing you to envision and materialize complex designs with ease.

2. Intuitive Division and Extraction

The Shape Builder Tool's power extends beyond merging—it empowers you to divide shapes, creating new forms with precision. By clicking on a shape within an overlapping area, you can segment it from the surrounding elements.

This feature is invaluable for creating custom icons, detailed illustrations, and complex textures. The ability to extract specific shapes from larger compositions opens the door to a myriad of design possibilities.

3. Freestyle Creation with the Paintbrush Gesture

In addition to its traditional drag-and-release functionality, the Shape Builder Tool offers a paintbrush gesture option. This mode allows you to intuitively draw over shapes you want to combine or divide, providing an even more natural and fluid creative process.

This freestyle approach invites experimentation, enabling you to create organic and expressive designs. Whether you're crafting hand-drawn icons or intricate abstract art, the paintbrush gesture adds a touch of artistic spontaneity.

4. Refinement and Iteration

The Shape Builder Tool is not just about initial creation—it's a tool for refinement and iteration. Once you've combined or divided shapes, you can continue to fine-tune your design by adjusting anchor points, curves, and paths.

This iterative process grants you the freedom to explore various design directions without being constrained by the initial shapes. It encourages a playful yet deliberate approach to design, ensuring that your final composition is a true reflection of your creative vision.

Elevating Designs with Precision and Innovation
The Shape Builder Tool is more than a feature; it's a gateway to innovation. It transcends the limitations of traditional shape creation, allowing you to imagine, experiment, and create in ways that were previously unimaginable.

By merging shapes, you can effortlessly craft intricate patterns and textured designs. Through division and extraction, you can customize forms to fit your unique vision. The paintbrush gesture unleashes your creative spontaneity, while the refinement phase ensures your designs are polished and perfected.

In Conclusion
The Shape Builder Tool in Adobe Illustrator is your creative ally, a tool that empowers you to transform simple shapes into intricate designs with a single click or gesture. It's not just about efficiency—it's about pushing the boundaries of design, exploring

uncharted territories, and achieving innovative outcomes.

As you wield the Shape Builder Tool, remember that its true power lies in your creativity. Embrace experimentation, celebrate unexpected results, and let your imagination guide you. With this tool at your disposal, you possess the ability to craft designs that are both visually stunning and conceptually groundbreaking. Let the Shape Builder Tool be your key to unlocking a new realm of artistic possibility, where each click and gesture becomes a stroke of brilliance on the canvas of creativity.

CHAPTER 3: VECTOR ARTISTRY UNLEASHED UNDERSTANDING VECTOR GRAPHICS AND THEIR ADVANTAGES

In the realm of digital design, the distinction between raster and vector graphics is profound. While both play a pivotal role in visual creation, vector graphics emerge as a dynamic and versatile medium that transcends the confines of pixels. In this article, we delve deep into the world of vector graphics, unraveling their intricacies and highlighting the myriad advantages they offer to artists, designers, and creators.

Understanding Vector Graphics: The Essence of Precision

At its core, a vector graphic is not composed of pixels but of mathematical equations that define lines, curves, shapes, and colors. This mathematical foundation grants vector graphics their unique characteristics and empowers designers to create images that are infinitely scalable without any loss of quality.

1. Scalability Without Limits

The defining feature of vector graphics is their ability to scale infinitely without compromising quality. Whether you're creating a small logo or a billboard-sized banner, vector graphics ensure that your design remains sharp, crisp, and visually appealing.

This scalability is achieved through the use of anchor points, curves, and lines that maintain their mathematical proportions regardless of size. As a result, vector graphics are ideal for projects that require flexibility and adaptability.

2. Precision and Consistency

Vectors are the architects of precision. With anchor points and Bezier handles, designers can manipulate shapes and lines with unparalleled accuracy. This precision lends itself to creating intricate designs, detailed illustrations, and geometric patterns that demand perfection.

Additionally, vector graphics enable visual consistency across different sizes and formats. Your design retains its proportions and quality, ensuring that your brand identity remains intact regardless of where it's displayed.

3. Small File Sizes

While raster graphics store visual information for each pixel, vector graphics store mathematical data. This fundamental difference results in smaller file sizes for vector images. As a result, vector graphics are ideal for web design, where quick loading times are crucial.

Smaller file sizes also make vector graphics suitable for digital distribution, whether through email, online platforms, or presentations. This efficiency enhances the overall user experience and minimizes storage concerns.

4. Edibility and Flexibility
Vector graphics are not static images; they're malleable compositions that can be easily edited and adapted. Each element—whether it's a line, shape, or color—can be adjusted individually, offering a level of flexibility that raster graphics can't match.

This editability extends beyond resizing. You can change colors, modify shapes, and even restructure entire compositions without compromising quality. This flexibility empowers designers to explore creative iterations and respond to client feedback swiftly.

Applications Across Diverse Domains
The advantages of vector graphics ripple through various creative domains, each benefiting from the precision and adaptability that vectors offer.

1. Logo Design and Branding
Vector graphics are the lifeblood of logos and branding materials. They ensure that your logo looks pristine across business cards, websites, billboards, and merchandise. The ability to scale without distortion guarantees brand recognition and consistency.

2. Illustration and Art

For illustrators and artists, vector graphics are an avenue for detail and complexity. The ability to manipulate individual anchor points and lines allows for the creation of intricate, lifelike illustrations that captivate the eye.

3. Typography and Layout Design

In typography and layout design, vectors facilitate the alignment of text, images, and elements with pixel-perfect precision. The scalability of vector text ensures legibility across various formats and screen sizes.

4. Engineering and Architectural Drafting

Beyond the realm of art and design, vector graphics find applications in engineering and architectural drafting. They enable the creation of precise blueprints and technical diagrams that communicate intricate details effectively.

In Conclusion

The world of vector graphics is a universe of precision, adaptability, and creativity. It's a realm where anchor points and mathematical equations become the building blocks of imagination. As you navigate the intricate landscape of digital design, remember that vector graphics are your passport to a boundless realm where size, quality, and creativity know no bounds.

Whether you're crafting a logo that defines a brand's identity, weaving intricate illustrations that tell captivating stories, or engineering technical diagrams that guide innovation, vector graphics empower you to shape your vision with unparalleled precision and creativity. Embrace the advantages they offer, and let vector graphics be your conduit to unlocking a world of limitless possibilities in the realm of digital creation.

ADVANCED TECHNIQUES FOR CREATING INTRICATE VECTOR ARTWORK

In the realm of digital design, intricate vector artwork stands as a testament to the artist's skill, creativity, and mastery of the medium. Beyond the basics of shapes and lines, advanced techniques elevate designs to a level of complexity that captivates the eye and engages the imagination. In this article, we embark on a journey through the realm of advanced techniques for creating intricate vector artwork, exploring the tools, strategies, and artistic choices that bring intricate designs to life.

1. Layered Complexity: The Art of Depth
One of the cornerstones of intricate vector artwork lies in the mastery of layering. By stacking elements and defining their order, you create depth and dimension within your composition. This layering technique adds complexity and visual interest, inviting viewers to explore your artwork with curiosity.

Start with a background layer that establishes the setting, then build upon it with foreground elements. This layering strategy creates a sense of depth, as objects appear to overlap and interact within the visual space. By experimenting with transparency, opacity, and blending modes, you can achieve stunning visual effects that breathe life into your designs.

2. Gradient Mesh: Crafting Photorealism

The Gradient Mesh tool is a powerhouse for achieving photorealistic effects within vector artwork. It enables you to create intricate shading and highlights that mimic the interplay of light and shadow on real-world surfaces. This technique is particularly valuable when crafting detailed portraits, objects, or scenes that demand a high level of realism.

To master the Gradient Mesh tool, start with basic shapes and gradually refine your mesh points to capture subtle variations in color and tone. By meticulously adjusting the anchor points within the mesh, you can achieve astonishing levels of detail and achieve an uncanny resemblance to reality.

3. Complex Clipping Masks: Concealing and Revealing

Clipping masks are a versatile tool for creating intricate designs by concealing and revealing specific parts of your artwork. By using shapes or objects as masks, you can achieve effects that fuse textures, patterns, and imagery seamlessly.

Experiment with intricate patterns and textures to add depth and complexity to your compositions. Overlaying these elements with clipping masks creates a harmonious blend that draws the viewer's attention and adds a tactile quality to your artwork.

4. Vector Brushes: Emulating Realistic Textures

Vector brushes are a secret weapon for infusing your artwork with texture and depth. Whether you're aiming for the look of hand-drawn illustrations, watercolor strokes, or intricate patterns, vector brushes offer a dynamic way to emulate a wide range of artistic mediums.

Customize vector brushes to suit your design's theme and style. By adjusting brush settings like size, scatter, and rotation, you can craft strokes that resemble natural textures while maintaining the scalability and precision of vector graphics.

5. Detail-Oriented Typography: Typography as Art

Typography is not confined to text—it's an essential element of design that can be turned into a masterpiece of its own. Combining intricate letterforms, ligatures, and decorative elements can transform typography into an artistic statement.

Experiment with custom lettering, embellishments, and flourishes to create intricate typographic compositions. Let each character interact with the others, and use details to guide the viewer's eye through your design with a sense of rhythm and harmony.

Conclusion: A Tapestry of Mastery
Intricate vector artwork is a tapestry woven from skill, creativity, and advanced techniques. Layering, gradient meshes, complex clipping masks, vector brushes, and detail-oriented typography are tools that help you build complexity, depth, and visual intrigue.

As you venture into the realm of advanced techniques, remember that mastery is a journey, not a destination. Embrace experimentation, push your creative boundaries, and let your passion for design guide your choices. With each stroke, each layer, and each intricate detail, you're crafting a masterpiece that invites viewers to explore, marvel, and appreciate the artistry that resides within the world of intricate vector artwork.

LEVERAGING GRADIENTS, PATTERNS, AND BLENDS TO ADD DEPTH

In the realm of visual communication, depth is a powerful tool that transforms flat designs into immersive artworks that captivate the viewer's gaze.

Among the arsenal of techniques at a designer's disposal, the strategic use of gradients, patterns, and blends stands as a cornerstone for adding depth and dimension to vector designs. In this article, we delve into the art of leveraging gradients, patterns, and blends to create a three-dimensional world within the confines of two-dimensional vector art.

1. The Power of Gradients: Crafting Realistic Transitions

Gradients are more than a simple progression of color—they're a gateway to visual depth. By transitioning smoothly between hues, gradients mimic the interplay of light and shadow on physical surfaces, infusing your designs with a sense of realism.

Creating Depth with Linear Gradients

Linear gradients are a versatile tool for simulating depth. By adjusting the angle and length of the gradient, you can create the illusion of light falling on objects from a specific direction. Incorporate gradients into backgrounds, shapes, and typography to achieve a sense of volume and three-dimensionality.

Radial Gradients: The Illusion of Depth and Focus

Radial gradients radiate from a central point, mimicking the way light interacts with convex and concave surfaces. By placing the brightest point at the center and gradually transitioning to darker shades, you can give objects a sense of curvature or a focal point that draws the viewer's attention.

2. Patterns: Texture and Complexity
Patterns are a design asset that lends a tactile quality to vector artwork. They're not only about aesthetics; they're about adding texture, intricacy, and depth to your compositions.

Imitating Natural Textures
Use patterns to simulate the textures found in the physical world—be it the grain of wood, the weave of fabric, or the surface of a stone. Applying these patterns to objects and backgrounds infuses your designs with a tangible quality that invites viewers to explore and engage.

Patterns for Illusion and Detail
Patterns can also create the illusion of depth and detail. By applying intricate patterns to different areas of your design, you can mimic complex surfaces or evoke a sense of richness. This technique is particularly useful for adding depth to architectural renderings, product designs, and nature-inspired artwork.

3. The Art of Blends: Smooth Transitions and Gradations
Blends are a dynamic tool for creating smooth transitions between shapes, colors, and sizes. They

allow you to craft seamless progressions that imbue your designs with a sense of continuity and depth.

Gradient Blends for Subtle Transition
Gradient blends enable you to create transitions that feel organic and fluid. Use them to simulate gradual changes in color, light, or texture. Whether it's a background that transitions from dawn to dusk or the shading on a three-dimensional object, gradient blends provide a gentle touch of realism.

Shape Blends: Creating Complex Forms
Shape blends go beyond colors—they allow you to create complex forms by transitioning between different shapes. By blending between circles and squares, or curves and polygons, you can craft intricate designs that appear to evolve organically, adding a layer of visual intrigue to your artwork.

Conclusion: A World of Depth and Creativity
The strategic use of gradients, patterns, and blends is your ticket to creating vector designs that transcend their two-dimensional nature. By mastering these techniques, you're not just adding depth; you're crafting a multidimensional experience that engages the viewer's senses and imagination.

As you experiment with gradients that mimic light, patterns that add texture, and blends that smooth transitions, remember that depth is not solely about visual tricks—it's about storytelling. It's about guiding the viewer's eye, creating focal points, and evoking emotions through the interplay of light and shadow.

In the world of vector design, depth is more than an illusion—it's an art form. Embrace the potential of gradients, patterns, and blends, and let them be your tools for sculpting a world that invites viewers to explore, appreciate, and immerse themselves in the rich tapestry of your vector creations.

CHAPTER 4: PRECISION TYPOGRAPHY
EXPLORING ADVANCED TYPOGRAPHY TOOLS AND TECHNIQUES

Typography isn't just about words; it's an art form that shapes the way we perceive and interact with visual content. While basic font selection is important, the world of typography holds advanced tools and techniques that allow designers to create captivating, expressive, and impactful designs. In this article, we delve into the realm of advanced typography, exploring the tools and techniques that transform letters into art and communication into a visual journey.

1. Kerning and Letter Spacing: Precision and Harmony

Kerning goes beyond selecting a font—it's the art of adjusting the space between individual letters to achieve optimal visual harmony. While most fonts come with default kerning, adjusting it manually can make a substantial difference in the overall legibility and aesthetic appeal of your text.

Mastering Kerning

Kerning is about creating consistent spacing between letters to eliminate awkward gaps or collisions. Pay attention to pairs of letters that often cause issues, such as "AV," "WA," or "TO." With subtle adjustments, you can achieve a polished and professional typographic appearance that ensures every word flows seamlessly.

2. Ligatures: Elevating Aesthetic and Readability

Ligatures are special characters that combine two or more letters into a single, more visually pleasing glyph. They serve to improve the aesthetics and readability of specific letter combinations that might otherwise clash.

Enhancing Aesthetics

Ligatures bring a touch of elegance and uniqueness to your typography. They're particularly useful in script fonts or calligraphy-inspired typefaces, where certain letter combinations benefit from the fluidity of a ligature.

3. OpenType Features: Hidden Gems of Typography

Modern fonts often come packed with OpenType features that allow for intricate typographic control. These features include stylistic alternates, swashes, titling capitals, and more—each contributing to the overall character of your design.

Customization and Expression

By accessing these OpenType features, you can tailor your typography to suit your design's personality. Swap out characters for alternatives that better fit your aesthetic vision, or add swashes to elevate the overall elegance of your text.

4. Variable Fonts: Dynamic Typography

Variable fonts are a revolutionary addition to the world of typography. Unlike traditional fonts that offer fixed styles (e.g., bold, italic), variable fonts allow for dynamic changes in weight, width, slant, and more—all within a single font file.

Responsive and Versatile Design

Variable fonts are a game-changer for responsive design, as they enable you to maintain consistent typographic aesthetics across various screen sizes and devices. They also empower designers to experiment with dynamic typography that adapts to different contexts without the need for multiple font files.

5. Hand Lettering and Custom Typography: Artistry and Originality

Taking typography to the next level involves crafting your own letterforms. Hand lettering and custom typography enable you to infuse your designs with originality, personality, and a human touch.

Creating Unique Letterforms

Hand lettering allows you to craft letterforms from scratch, tailoring them to suit the mood and message of your design. This technique is particularly valuable for branding, packaging, and projects that demand a distinct visual identity.

Conclusion: Crafting Type as Art

Advanced typography isn't just about selecting fonts—it's a journey into the realm of artistry, expression, and precision. By mastering tools like kerning and ligatures, you fine-tune the aesthetics and readability of your text. OpenType features and variable fonts give you unparalleled typographic control and adaptability. Hand lettering and custom typography transform letters into artistic forms that embody your unique creative vision.

Typography is the voice of your design. It guides the reader's eye, communicates emotions, and enhances the overall aesthetic. As you navigate the world of advanced typography, remember that each decision—from kerning adjustments to custom lettering—shapes the narrative of your design. Embrace the tools and techniques that typography offers, and let them be your instruments for creating designs that speak volumes, not just in words, but in artful expression.

CREATING CUSTOM TYPE DESIGNS AND LAYOUTS

Typography is more than just a conveyance of words; it's a visual language that communicates emotions, narratives, and aesthetics. While pre-existing fonts are widely available, the world of design holds a treasure trove of creativity in crafting custom type designs and layouts. In this article, we embark on a journey into the realm of custom typography, exploring the tools, techniques, and artistic decisions that transform letters into intricate works of art and layouts into captivating visual stories.

1. Handcrafted Letterforms: Infusing Personality and Authenticity

Handcrafted letterforms add a touch of authenticity and uniqueness to your designs. By creating custom typefaces, you're not just selecting characters from a font menu—you're shaping an entire alphabet to resonate with your project's identity.

Starting with Sketches

Begin with pen and paper, sketching out different letterforms and experimenting with styles. This phase is where you let your creativity flow, exploring a range of shapes and strokes that capture the essence of your design.

Translating to Digital Medium

Once you have a set of hand-drawn characters, bring them into digital software for refinement. Vector-based programs like Adobe Illustrator allow you to recreate and adjust your letterforms while maintaining scalability and precision.

2. Balancing Aesthetics and Readability

Creating custom typefaces is an art of balance—between aesthetics and readability, between form and function. While expressive and ornate characters may add visual flair, it's crucial to ensure that the type remains legible and accessible to your audience.

Considering Context and Usage

The context in which your custom typeface will be used plays a significant role in shaping its design. A typeface for a wedding invitation may have a different aesthetic than one for a technical report. Adapt the style to suit the message and mood of the design.

3. Exploring Layouts: Harmonizing Type and Composition

Designing custom type layouts involves more than arranging words—it's about orchestrating an ensemble of type, imagery, and negative space that tells a cohesive visual story.

Hierarchy and Emphasis

Consider the hierarchy of information and use type size, weight, and color to guide the reader's eye. Headlines, subheadings, and body text should work harmoniously to convey the intended message.

Whitespace as a Design Element

Whitespace, or negative space, is as important as the text itself. Properly utilized whitespace helps to prevent visual clutter and allows the eye to rest, enhancing the overall readability and aesthetics of the layout.

4. Typography and Branding: Unifying Visual Identity

Custom type designs and layouts play a pivotal role in branding. They provide a unique visual identity that sets a brand apart from its competitors.

Creating Branded Typography

Developing a custom typeface exclusively for your brand infuses it with personality and memorability. This typeface becomes a recognizable mark, embodying your brand's values and aesthetics.

Consistency Across Platforms

Consistency in typography across various platforms—print materials, websites, social media—is vital for reinforcing your brand's identity. Custom type designs and layouts ensure that your branding remains cohesive and recognizable.

Conclusion: The Art of Expression

Custom typography and layouts are not just design elements; they're the embodiments of creativity, intention, and artistic expression. By crafting letterforms that resonate with your project's identity, you create visual language unique to your message. By designing layouts that harmonize type and imagery, you orchestrate a symphony of visual storytelling.

As you navigate the world of custom type designs and layouts, remember that every stroke, every alignment, and every choice of typeface serves a purpose. Whether you're creating a brand identity, a magazine spread, or a digital interface, custom typography and layouts elevate your designs from mere words to captivating visual narratives. Embrace the tools and techniques that design offers, and let them be your guide in shaping a world where type and layout come together as an artful expression of creativity and communication.

WORKING WITH TEXT ON PATHS AND WITHIN SHAPES

Typography isn't confined to straight lines and static layouts. In the dynamic world of design, text has the power to curve, flow, and adapt to the contours of shapes, adding a new dimension of creativity to visual communication. In this article, we delve into the art of working with text on paths and within shapes, exploring techniques that transform words into design elements that capture attention and engage the viewer.

1. Text on Paths: Curving Words with Artistry

Text on paths is a technique that takes typography beyond the confines of horizontal lines. By curving text along custom paths, you create visual interest and guide the viewer's gaze in a fluid and engaging manner.

Curved Paths for Expressive Typography

Using software like Adobe Illustrator, you can easily create custom paths for your text to follow. These paths can take the shape of arcs, circles, or even intricate freeform lines. This technique is particularly useful for crafting headlines, logos, and designs that demand an element of dynamism.

Balance and Readability

While curving text adds a dynamic touch, it's crucial to maintain readability. Adjust the spacing and font size to ensure that the text remains clear and legible. Experiment with various alignments and curves to strike a balance between visual impact and clarity.

2. Text Within Shapes: Filling Forms with Expression

Placing text within shapes transforms letters into design elements that complement the overall composition. Whether it's filling a logo with a company name or integrating text into an illustration, this technique adds depth and unity to your designs.

Creating Effective Text Shapes

Choose shapes that resonate with your design's message and mood. The shape should enhance the text's readability and evoke the desired emotional response. For instance, using flowing text within a heart shape can evoke feelings of romance and warmth.

Maintaining Balance and Contrast

When placing text within shapes, consider the contrast between the text color and the shape's color. Ensure that the text remains visible and legible against the background. Experiment with opacity and blending modes to achieve the desired effect.

3. Practical Applications: Logos, Banners, and More

The techniques of text on paths and within shapes have numerous practical applications across various design projects.

Creative Logos

Designing logos with text on paths or within shapes infuses them with a unique visual identity. The typography becomes an integral part of the logo's design, reinforcing brand recognition and memorability.

Engaging Banners and Posters

Text on paths can be particularly effective in banners and posters, where it guides the viewer's eye along a specific visual path. Use curved text to highlight key messages or draw attention to important elements within the design.

Expressive Typography Art

These techniques also open doors to expressive typography art. By experimenting with different shapes, paths, and text placements, you can create captivating typographic compositions that tell visual stories.

Conclusion: Typography as Dynamic Expression

Typography is an art form that thrives on flexibility and expression. Working with text on paths and within shapes allows you to bend, twist, and mold words into captivating design elements. This dynamic approach to typography adds layers of depth, engagement, and creativity to your designs.

As you embrace the art of curving text along paths and integrating it within shapes, remember that each choice you make contributes to the overall visual impact and narrative of your design. Whether you're crafting a logo, a poster, or a piece of typographic art, let the techniques of text manipulation become your instruments for transforming words into dynamic expressions that captivate the viewer's eye and ignite the imagination.

CHAPTER 5: ADVANCED BLENDING AND MASKING
HARNESSING THE POTENTIAL OF BLENDING MODES AND OPACITY SETTINGS

In the realm of visual design, achieving captivating compositions goes beyond arranging elements on a canvas. Blending modes and opacity settings are powerful tools that elevate designs from the ordinary to the extraordinary. In this article, we embark on a journey through the realm of blending modes and opacity settings, unveiling their potential to transform visual elements, evoke emotions, and infuse designs with depth and intrigue.

1. Blending Modes: A Symphony of Visual Harmony
Blending modes are a set of mathematical algorithms that dictate how colors interact when layers overlap. They provide a spectrum of possibilities, allowing you to create effects that range from subtle enhancements to dramatic transformations.

Overlay and Multiply: Creating Depth and Contrast
The "Overlay" blending mode infuses colors with vibrancy and contrast, making images pop. Use it to intensify shadows and highlights, adding depth and dimension to your designs. On the other hand, the "Multiply" blending mode darkens underlying layers, contributing to a moody atmosphere and creating a sense of depth.

Screen and Lighten: Illuminating Effects

"Screen" and "Lighten" blending modes create luminous effects by brightening underlying layers. These modes are ideal for achieving soft glows, radiant highlights, and ethereal light effects. They're particularly useful for adding a touch of magic to fantasy-themed designs and dreamy atmospheres.

2. Opacity: The Art of Transparency and Depth

Opacity settings allow you to control the transparency of layers, creating a sense of depth, subtlety, and focus within your compositions.

Gradual Fading with Reduced Opacity

Reducing the opacity of an element can create a gradual fading effect that draws the viewer's attention to other focal points. This technique is valuable for designing user interfaces, where less important elements can fade into the background, allowing critical content to shine.

Layering for Textures and Complexity

Layering multiple elements with varying opacities can result in textured and intricate designs. By stacking semi-transparent layers, you can craft compositions that resemble collages, adding layers of visual interest and depth.

3. Practical Applications: From Photography to Digital Art

Blending modes and opacity settings have a myriad of applications that span across different design domains.

Photography Enhancement

In photo editing, blending modes and opacity settings breathe life into images. Apply them to achieve vintage effects, overlay textures, or intensify the mood of a photograph.

Digital Painting and Illustration

In digital painting and illustration, these tools enable artists to create rich textures, dynamic lighting, and atmospheric effects. They contribute to the overall mood and storytelling of the artwork.

Graphic Design and Marketing

In graphic design, blending modes and opacity settings can accentuate typography, enhance logos, and create captivating banners. They play a crucial role in conveying messages and emotions through visuals.

Conclusion: Illuminating Design Potential

Blending modes and opacity settings are more than technical tools; they're conduits for creativity and expression. As you delve into the world of design, remember that every choice you make with blending modes and opacity contributes to the narrative and aesthetic of your composition.

Whether you're crafting a surreal artwork, enhancing a photograph, or designing a user interface, let blending modes and opacity settings be your companions in shaping visual journeys that captivate, engage, and resonate with your audience. Embrace experimentation, celebrate the unexpected, and let the potential of these tools guide you in crafting designs that are not just visually pleasing, but emotionally evocative and artistically profound.

MASTERING COMPLEX MASKING TECHNIQUES FOR CREATIVE EFFECTS

Design is not just about aesthetics; it's a canvas for storytelling, emotion, and impact. Complex masking techniques are the artist's toolbox for transcending the boundaries of simple shapes and unleashing a world of creative effects. In this article, we delve into the art of mastering complex masking techniques, exploring how they empower designers to craft compositions that are dynamic, intriguing, and visually stunning.

1. Understanding Masking: The Art of Concealment and Revelation

Masking is the process of selectively revealing or concealing portions of an image or design element. It's a technique that allows designers to combine elements seamlessly, create intricate compositions, and achieve unique visual effects.

Layer Masks: Seamless Blending
Layer masks are fundamental to complex masking techniques. By applying a grayscale mask to a layer, you can control the visibility of specific parts. Painting on the mask with black conceals, while white reveals. This method enables you to blend images, textures, and objects with precision and subtlety.

Clipping Masks: Controlled Visibility
Clipping masks allow you to limit the visibility of one layer based on the content of another. This technique is particularly useful for placing an image within a specific shape or text, creating dynamic visuals that draw the viewer's eye.

2. Advanced Techniques: From Double Exposure to Intricate Textures
Complex masking techniques go beyond the basics, opening doors to a world of artistic exploration and innovation.

Double Exposure: Merging Worlds
Double exposure involves blending two or more images to create a surreal, harmonious composition. By using layer masks, you can seamlessly merge portraits with landscapes or objects, resulting in visually captivating and thought-provoking designs.

Texture Masking: Adding Depth and Detail
Texture masking is a technique that enhances the depth and character of your designs. By applying textured masks to images or backgrounds, you can achieve a tactile quality that evokes emotions and engages the viewer's senses.

3. Creativity Unleashed: Intricate Composite Art
Complex masking techniques shine in the realm of composite art, where multiple elements come together to form a unified visual narrative.

Collage Art: Crafting Visual Stories
Collage art involves assembling diverse elements into a cohesive composition. With masking, you can seamlessly blend photographs, illustrations, and textures, weaving a visual tapestry that tells a story or conveys an idea.

Surreal Art: Beyond Reality
Surreal art pushes the boundaries of reality, often with dreamlike or fantastical elements. Complex masking techniques enable you to juxtapose unrelated objects, manipulate perspectives, and create captivating scenes that challenge the viewer's perception.

Conclusion: Where Creativity and Skill Converge
Mastering complex masking techniques is a journey of creative expression and technical skill. By understanding layer masks, clipping masks, and

advanced methods, you unlock the potential to create designs that are not just aesthetically pleasing, but emotionally resonant and conceptually rich.

As you delve into the world of complex masking, remember that every brushstroke, every layer, and every choice contributes to the final composition. Embrace experimentation, embrace happy accidents, and let the techniques of masking become your tools for sculpting designs that are dynamic, immersive, and uniquely yours. Let your creativity soar as you explore the boundless possibilities that complex masking offers, transforming your designs into visual narratives that captivate, provoke, and inspire.

CREATING SEAMLESS COMPOSITIONS USING CLIPPING MASKS AND OPACITY MASKS

In the world of design, achieving seamless and harmonious compositions is a pursuit that combines technical finesse with artistic vision. Clipping masks and opacity masks are two powerful tools that empower designers to create captivating visuals that seamlessly merge elements, textures, and colors. In this article, we embark on a journey into the realm of clipping masks and opacity masks, unveiling their potential to craft compositions that are not just visually pleasing, but conceptually rich and emotionally resonant.

1. Clipping Masks: Enveloping Creativity with Precision

Clipping masks are a versatile technique that allows designers to constrain the visibility of one layer based on the shape of another layer. They enable you to fit images or elements into specific forms, creating dynamic compositions that engage the viewer's eye.

Creating Visual Depth

Clipping masks can be used to infuse depth into designs. By placing an image within a shape and adjusting its position, you create the illusion that the image exists within the boundaries of the shape, adding visual interest and dimension.

Text as Art: Typography with a Twist

Clipping masks can elevate typography from words on a page to visual art. By placing text within shapes or images, you mold letters into design elements that convey emotions, messages, and narratives beyond their literal meaning.

2. Opacity Masks: The Symphony of Transparency

Opacity masks offer a sophisticated way to control the transparency of elements within a design. This technique enables designers to create intricate blends, transitions, and visual effects that evoke emotions and captivate the viewer's gaze.

Transitions and Gradients: The Power of Smooth Blending

Opacity masks are ideal for creating seamless transitions between elements. By applying a gradient to an opacity mask, you can smoothly blend two images or colors, creating a mesmerizing visual effect that guides the eye along a path.

Textural Magic: Applying Opacity Masks to Textures

Opacity masks are a secret weapon for incorporating textures into designs. By applying an opacity mask to an image or layer, you can reveal or conceal specific parts, allowing textures to merge with backgrounds and elements to add depth and tactile quality.

3. Practical Applications: From Web Design to Digital Art

The applications of clipping masks and opacity masks are boundless, spanning across diverse design projects.

Web Design and User Interfaces

Clipping masks and opacity masks play a vital role in web design, allowing designers to create visually appealing user interfaces. By seamlessly blending images, icons, and text, you craft designs that are both functional and aesthetically pleasing.

Digital Art and Illustration

In digital art, these techniques are a gateway to creating mesmerizing visual effects and atmospheric compositions. Opacity masks, in particular, enable artists to add layers of complexity, lighting effects, and dreamlike qualities to their artwork.

Conclusion: The Craftsmanship of Seamless Design
Clipping masks and opacity masks are more than design tools; they're instruments for crafting compositions that are visually immersive, conceptually intriguing, and emotionally resonant. As you navigate the world of seamless compositions, remember that each choice you make with these techniques contributes to the overall narrative and aesthetics of your design.

Whether you're integrating text within shapes, blending images seamlessly, or applying intricate opacity masks to textures, let these techniques be your allies in shaping designs that engage, enchant, and evoke emotions. Embrace the potential they offer, and let your creativity unfold as you explore the endless possibilities of clipping masks and opacity masks, transforming your designs into artful expressions that captivate the eye and stir the soul.

CHAPTER 6: 3D EFFECTS AND PERSPECTIVE INTRODUCING ILLUSTRATOR'S 3D CAPABILITIES FOR DYNAMIC DESIGNS

Design is an ever-evolving art that thrives on pushing boundaries and breaking free from the constraints of the two-dimensional realm. Adobe Illustrator's 3D capabilities offer designers a gateway to a new dimension—one where objects can be sculpted, rotated, and illuminated to create dynamic and captivating visuals. In this article, we embark on a journey into the world of Adobe Illustrator's 3D capabilities, exploring how they empower designers to craft compositions that transcend flatness and embrace depth, perspective, and realism.

1. The Art of Extrusion: Shaping Depth and Dimension

Extrusion is a fundamental 3D technique that transforms 2D shapes into three-dimensional objects. It involves pulling a 2D shape along an axis to create depth and volume. The result is a visual interplay of light and shadow that adds a sense of realism and depth to your designs.

Creating 3D Text and Logos

Adobe Illustrator's 3D capabilities allow you to transform text and logos into sculpted forms that appear to leap off the page. By applying extrusion, you give these elements depth and presence, making them stand out in the visual space.

2. The Power of Rotation: Dynamic Perspectives

Rotation is a cornerstone of 3D design that allows you to manipulate objects from various angles. Adobe Illustrator enables you to rotate objects on different axes, creating dynamic compositions that engage the viewer's eye.

Creating Compelling Packaging Designs

3D rotation is a valuable tool for designing packaging and product mockups. By showcasing products from different perspectives, you provide clients and consumers with a comprehensive view that highlights features and details.

3. Lighting and Shading: Infusing Realism and Drama

Lighting and shading are integral to 3D design, as they emulate how light interacts with objects in the physical world. Adobe Illustrator's 3D capabilities enable you to adjust lighting angles, intensities, and colors, creating realistic highlights and shadows that lend depth and authenticity to your designs.

Enhancing Illustrations with Drama

Adobe Illustrator's 3D lighting options allow you to infuse your illustrations with drama and mood. By strategically placing light sources and adjusting their settings, you can create scenes that evoke emotions and captivate the viewer's imagination.

4. Practical Applications: From Digital Art to Product Visualization

The applications of Adobe Illustrator's 3D capabilities span across diverse design domains.

Digital Art and Illustration

In digital art, Adobe Illustrator's 3D capabilities expand your creative arsenal. You can create surreal scenes, fantastical landscapes, and intricate architectural structures that transport viewers into immersive visual worlds.

Product Visualization and Prototyping

For product designers, Adobe Illustrator's 3D capabilities offer a platform for creating realistic prototypes and visualizations. Whether you're designing consumer products or industrial machinery, these tools enable you to showcase concepts in a lifelike context.

Conclusion: A Dimensional Revolution in Design

Adobe Illustrator's 3D capabilities represent a revolution in design—one that invites designers to break free from the constraints of two-dimensionality and explore the rich realm of depth, perspective, and realism. As you delve into the world of 3D design, remember that each rotation, each extrusion, and each play of light contributes to the overall impact and narrative of your composition.

Whether you're sculpting 3D text, experimenting with lighting, or crafting product mockups, let Adobe Illustrator's 3D capabilities be your artistic playground. Embrace the potential they offer, and let your creativity soar as you explore the endless possibilities of three-dimensional design, transforming your concepts into dynamic, immersive, and visually compelling works of art that captivate the eye and ignite the imagination.

CREATING 3D OBJECTS, TEXT, AND EFFECTS

In the vast canvas of design, the incorporation of three-dimensional elements introduces a new layer of dynamism and realism. Creating 3D objects, text, and effects transcends the realm of flat imagery, allowing designers to shape visual narratives that leap off the page and into the viewer's imagination. In this article, we delve into the art of crafting 3D elements, exploring how designers can use tools and techniques to infuse depth, perspective, and impact into their creations.

1. Sculpting 3D Objects: Elevating Visual Presence
Designing 3D objects involves transforming two-dimensional shapes into tangible forms that interact with light and shadow. By mastering this technique, designers can create visually engaging compositions that simulate the tangible world.

Extrusion: Giving Depth to Shapes
Extrusion is a foundational technique for creating 3D objects. By pulling a 2D shape along an axis, you generate depth and volume. This technique is invaluable for shaping objects with texture, such as bottles, packaging, and architectural elements.

Beveling: Adding Realism to Edges
Beveling is the art of adding a chamfer or rounded edge to a 3D object. This technique mimics real-world lighting effects and enhances the object's realism. Beveled edges catch and reflect light, giving objects a polished and tactile appearance.

2. Crafting 3D Text: Breathing Life into Words
Text, when transformed into 3D, becomes more than mere characters—it becomes an integral part of the design, adding depth and emphasis to messages and narratives.

Extruding Text: From Flat to Dynamic
Extruding text elevates typography from the page to the realm of sculpted art. Designers can use this technique to create logos, headlines, and titles that command attention and convey the essence of the message.

Texturing and Lighting: Infusing Character
Applying textures and lighting effects to 3D text enhances its personality and impact. By experimenting with different materials and lighting

angles, designers can achieve effects ranging from glossy metallics to weathered wood.

3. Elevating Designs with 3D Effects: Visual Enchantment

Beyond objects and text, the strategic use of 3D effects can transform designs, adding visual enchantment and intrigue.

Drop Shadows and Reflections: Mimicking Reality

By incorporating realistic drop shadows and reflections, designers can anchor 3D objects within their environments. These effects create the illusion of objects interacting with surfaces, enhancing depth and grounding the design.

Depth of Field: Guiding the Viewer's Gaze

Depth of field is a technique that mimics the behavior of camera lenses. Designers can use it to focus attention on specific elements, blurring the background and creating a sense of depth that guides the viewer's gaze.

Practical Applications: From Branding to Digital Art

The applications of 3D elements in design are diverse, spanning across various design disciplines.

Branding and Logos

Designers can leverage 3D techniques to breathe life into logos, creating memorable visual identities that stand out in a crowded marketplace.

Digital Art and Visual Storytelling
In digital art, 3D elements enable designers to create immersive scenes, fantastical landscapes, and dynamic characters that engage the viewer's imagination.

Conclusion: Crafting Depth and Impact
Creating 3D objects, text, and effects is a journey of transforming imagination into tangible art. As designers navigate the world of three-dimensional design, every extrusion, bevel, and lighting adjustment becomes a brushstroke that contributes to the overall narrative and emotion of the composition.

Whether you're sculpting 3D objects for packaging, crafting 3D text for logos, or applying 3D effects to enhance visual impact, let these techniques be your tools for shaping designs that transcend flatness. Embrace the potential they offer, and let your creativity flow as you explore the boundless possibilities of 3D design, transforming your concepts into vibrant, multidimensional works of art that captivate the eye and resonate with the soul.

IMPLEMENTING PERSPECTIVE GRIDS FOR REALISTIC DEPTH

Design is a canvas where imagination meets reality, and the illusion of depth is a powerful tool to engage and captivate viewers. Perspective grids are the secret ingredient that brings this depth to life, allowing designers to create compositions that mimic the way we perceive the world around us. In this article, we delve into the art of implementing perspective grids, exploring how they infuse designs with realistic depth, dimension, and impact.

1. Understanding Perspective: The Gateway to Realism

Perspective is the visual technique that simulates depth and distance on a two-dimensional surface. By understanding the principles of linear and atmospheric perspective, designers can replicate the way objects appear smaller as they recede into the distance, creating a sense of realism.

Linear Perspective: Creating Vanishing Points

Linear perspective involves using vanishing points and lines to create the illusion of depth. Designers can establish vanishing points on the horizon line, which serves as the viewer's eye level. Lines radiating from these points determine the converging angles and relative sizes of objects.

Atmospheric Perspective: Capturing Distance

Atmospheric perspective involves simulating the way distant objects appear fainter, bluer, and less detailed due to atmospheric effects. By adjusting color saturation, contrast, and detail, designers can convey depth and distance, enhancing the realism of their compositions.

2. The Power of Perspective Grids: Crafting Realistic Depth

Perspective grids are the backbone of creating accurate and dynamic depth in designs. They provide a framework for aligning elements in accordance with perspective principles, enabling designers to construct compositions that appear three-dimensional.

Creating Perspective Grids

Design software like Adobe Illustrator offers tools to create custom perspective grids. These grids consist of intersecting lines that converge towards vanishing points, serving as guides for placing elements in a way that aligns with the intended perspective.

Placing Elements with Precision

Once the perspective grid is established, designers can place elements on the grid, ensuring that they follow the lines of convergence. This technique allows for accurate positioning and scaling of objects, resulting in a composition that adheres to realistic depth cues.

3. Practical Applications: From Architecture to Illustration

Perspective grids have diverse applications across various design disciplines.

Architectural Visualization

In architectural design, perspective grids are invaluable for creating accurate renderings of buildings and structures. Designers can use grids to establish proper proportions, spatial relationships, and viewpoints, resulting in realistic and compelling visualizations.

Illustration and Concept Art

In illustration, perspective grids serve as a foundation for constructing scenes with depth and dimension. Illustrators can use grids to create landscapes, interiors, and urban environments that draw viewers into the artwork's narrative.

Conclusion: Breathing Life into Flat Surfaces

Implementing perspective grids is a journey into the art of realism and dimension. As designers dive into the world of perspective, each line, each vanishing point, and each element placement contributes to the overall depth and authenticity of the composition.

Whether you're visualizing architectural designs or crafting captivating illustrations, let perspective grids be your guide to creating compositions that transcend flat surfaces. Embrace the principles they offer, and let your creativity flourish as you explore the endless possibilities of perspective, transforming your designs into multidimensional experiences that captivate the viewer's eye and transport them into a world of visual depth and realism.

CHAPTER 7: ADVANCED COLOR AND GRADIENT TECHNIQUES
DELVING INTO COLOR THEORY AND ITS APPLICATION IN ILLUSTRATOR

In the realm of design, color is more than just a visual element; it's a language that conveys emotions, messages, and identities. Understanding color theory and its application is a cornerstone of effective design, enabling designers to craft compositions that resonate with viewers on a profound level. In this article, we embark on a journey into the world of color theory, delving into its significance and exploring how it can be applied using Adobe Illustrator to create visually captivating and emotionally impactful designs.

1. The Essence of Color Theory: A Palette of Emotions
Color theory is the study of how colors interact, evoke emotions, and communicate messages. By comprehending the psychology of colors, designers can select hues that align with the intended mood, tone, and narrative of their designs.

Primary, Secondary, and Tertiary Colors
Color theory begins with an understanding of the color wheel, which consists of primary colors (red, blue, yellow), secondary colors (green, orange, purple), and tertiary colors (combinations of primary and secondary colors). The relationships between these colors form the foundation of color harmony.

Color Temperature and Emotion

Colors are often categorized into warm and cool tones. Warm colors, like red and orange, evoke feelings of warmth, energy, and passion. Cool colors, like blue and green, evoke feelings of calmness, tranquility, and serenity. Designers can leverage these associations to create desired emotional responses in viewers.

2. Applying Color Theory in Adobe Illustrator: Tools and Techniques

Adobe Illustrator provides a comprehensive toolkit for applying color theory to design projects. From selecting color schemes to creating gradients, the software empowers designers to bring color theories to life.

Color Harmony and Schemes

Adobe Illustrator offers color harmony rules that help designers select harmonious color combinations. Analogous, complementary, and triadic color schemes are just a few options that ensure color choices work well together.

Creating Color Palettes

Illustrator's Color Themes panel enables designers to extract color palettes from images and artwork, providing a starting point for designs. These palettes can then be customized and applied to elements within the composition.

3. Embracing Color Psychology: The Art of Message Conveyance

Color psychology is the study of how colors influence human behavior and emotions. Designers can leverage this knowledge to ensure their color choices align with the intended message and impact of their designs.

Branding and Identity

Colors play a crucial role in branding and identity. By selecting colors that resonate with a brand's values and personality, designers can create visual identities that are instantly recognizable and memorable.

Cultural and Contextual Considerations

Different cultures and contexts attribute varying meanings to colors. For instance, while white represents purity in Western cultures, it symbolizes mourning in some Eastern cultures. Designers must consider these cultural nuances to ensure their designs are culturally sensitive and universally understood.

Conclusion: The Language of Color Mastery

Color theory is a language that transcends words, enabling designers to communicate emotions, ideas, and stories through visuals. As designers explore the world of color theory, each hue, shade, and combination becomes a brushstroke that contributes to the overall impact and resonance of the composition.

Whether you're creating brand identities, illustrations, or user interfaces, let color theory be your guide. Embrace the principles it offers, and let Adobe Illustrator be your canvas for translating theories into captivating designs. By harmonizing colors, understanding their psychological effects, and aligning them with the intended message, you can transform your designs into vibrant visual narratives that speak directly to the heart and mind of the viewer.

CREATING AND USING CUSTOM COLOR SWATCHES AND LIBRARIES

Colors are the building blocks of visual expression, and custom color swatches and libraries serve as the artist's palette, offering a spectrum of possibilities to paint vibrant compositions. In the realm of design, these tools are invaluable for maintaining consistency, conveying brand identity, and unleashing creative expression. In this article, we delve into the art of creating and using custom color swatches and libraries, exploring how they empower designers to infuse their work with cohesion, personality, and innovation.

1. Custom Color Swatches: A Canvas of Possibilities
Custom color swatches are collections of colors curated to suit a particular project, brand, or aesthetic. By creating and utilizing these swatches,

designers ensure visual harmony and streamline the color-selection process.

Creating Custom Swatches
Design software like Adobe Illustrator enables designers to create custom color swatches from scratch. They can use the software's color picker to select hues manually, input RGB or CMYK values, or even import colors from existing images.

Consistency and Brand Identity
Custom color swatches are invaluable for maintaining consistency in design projects. Brands can establish a unique color palette that becomes synonymous with their identity, facilitating instant recognition among audiences.

2. Building Color Libraries: A Repository of Inspiration
Color libraries are collections of custom color swatches that can be accessed and applied across various projects. They serve as a repository of inspiration, enabling designers to reuse successful color combinations and maintain a cohesive visual language.

Saving and Managing Color Libraries
Design software allows designers to save and manage custom color libraries. These libraries can be named, organized, and accessed whenever needed. This feature is particularly useful for agencies, studios, or

designers working on multiple projects simultaneously.

Cross-Project Cohesion
Color libraries foster cohesion across diverse projects. By utilizing consistent color schemes, designers create a unified visual identity that strengthens brand recognition and resonates with viewers.

3. Application and Benefits: From Branding to Illustration
Custom color swatches and libraries have a wide array of applications across various design disciplines.

Branding and Marketing
In branding and marketing, custom color swatches ensure that designs align with the brand's personality and convey a consistent message. This consistency enhances brand recognition and fosters a sense of trust and familiarity.

Illustration and Art
Custom color swatches and libraries provide illustrators with a toolset to infuse their artwork with unique palettes. This creative freedom enables illustrators to experiment with colors and moods, bringing their visual narratives to life.

Conclusion: Colors Unleashed, Creativity Amplified
Custom color swatches and libraries are the designer's gateway to unleashing the full potential of color in their work. As designers explore these tools, each color choice becomes a stroke of creativity that contributes to the overall mood, impact, and resonance of the composition.

Whether you're crafting branding materials, illustrating visual stories, or designing user interfaces, let custom color swatches and libraries be your guide. Embrace the power they offer, and let them amplify your creative expression in software like Adobe Illustrator. By curating harmonious palettes, maintaining brand identity, and infusing designs with personality, you can transform your projects into vibrant visual journeys that captivate the eye, communicate messages, and evoke emotions.

BLENDING AND MESHING GRADIENTS FOR CAPTIVATING VISUAL EFFECTS

In the realm of design, the ability to seamlessly blend colors and create mesmerizing transitions is a hallmark of artistic finesse. Blending and meshing gradients are techniques that empower designers to craft compositions that evoke emotions, depth, and intrigue. In this article, we delve into the world of gradient blending and meshing, uncovering their potential to transform designs into captivating visual spectacles that captivate the eye and stimulate the imagination.

1. Understanding Gradients: A Spectrum of Possibilities

Gradients are a spectrum of colors that transition smoothly from one hue to another. These transitions can be subtle or dramatic, creating visual interest and adding dimension to designs.

Linear Gradients: Subtle Elegance

Linear gradients involve a smooth transition from one color to another along a straight line. Designers can control the angle and length of the transition, creating elegant and understated effects that enhance the overall composition.

Radial Gradients: Circular Radiance

Radial gradients emanate from a central point, radiating outward. They can create the illusion of light and depth, making them ideal for simulating light sources, glowing effects, and highlighting focal points.

2. Mastering Gradient Blending: Harmonious Transitions

Gradient blending is the art of seamlessly transitioning between different colors, creating compositions that flow and meld harmoniously.

Creating Smooth Transitions

Designers can use gradient blending to create smooth transitions between colors, achieving effects that range from soft and ethereal to dynamic and vibrant. By choosing colors that complement each other, designers create compositions that are visually captivating and emotionally resonant.

Depth and Dimension

Gradient blending can simulate depth and dimension, making objects appear more three-dimensional. By applying gradients to backgrounds, designers create the illusion of depth, making foreground elements pop off the canvas.

3. Meshing Gradients: Sculpting Complex Forms

Meshing gradients take blending to a new level by allowing designers to apply gradients to complex shapes, resulting in intricate and nuanced visual effects.

Applying Gradients to Shapes

Meshing involves applying gradients to vector shapes, allowing designers to create the illusion of three-dimensional forms. Each point in the mesh can be individually manipulated, enabling designers to sculpt gradients to fit the contours of the shape.

Creating Realistic Textures

Meshing gradients can replicate realistic textures, such as fur, fabric, or organic surfaces. Designers can manipulate points within the mesh to mimic the play of light on intricate textures, adding a tactile quality to their designs.

Practical Applications: From Digital Art to User Interfaces

Gradient blending and meshing find application across diverse design domains.

Digital Art and Illustration

In digital art, gradient blending and meshing enable artists to create atmospheric effects, dynamic lighting, and surreal compositions. These techniques contribute to the mood, storytelling, and overall impact of the artwork.

User Interface and Web Design

In user interface and web design, gradient blending and meshing can add depth and interactivity to interfaces. Subtle gradients can guide users' attention and create hierarchy, enhancing the user experience.

Conclusion: Crafting Visual Symphony

Gradient blending and meshing are the instruments that enable designers to compose visual symphonies. As designers explore these techniques, each color transition, each gradient application, and each mesh manipulation contributes to the overall harmony and resonance of the composition.

Whether you're crafting digital artwork, designing user interfaces, or creating illustrations, let gradient blending and meshing be your tools for orchestrating captivating visual effects. Embrace their potential, and let them guide your creative expression in software like Adobe Illustrator. By seamlessly blending colors, sculpting gradients to fit shapes, and experimenting with textures, you can transform your designs into captivating visual narratives that invite viewers to explore, experience, and immerse themselves in a world of breathtaking visual spectacle.

CHAPTER 8: ARTBOARDS AND ADVANCED LAYOUTS MAXIMIZING EFFICIENCY WITH MULTIPLE ARTBOARDS

In the ever-evolving landscape of design, efficiency is paramount. The ability to seamlessly manage multiple design iterations, concepts, and formats is a hallmark of a skilled designer. Multiple artboards are a game-changing tool that empowers designers to streamline their workflow, enhance organization, and embrace versatility. In this article, we delve into the realm of multiple artboards, uncovering their potential to maximize efficiency and transform the design process into a symphony of creativity and order.

1. A Canvas of Possibilities: Understanding Multiple Artboards

Multiple artboards are like pages within a single document. They allow designers to work on multiple iterations, concepts, or formats within one cohesive project file. This feature is particularly valuable for projects with various design elements, sizes, or versions.

Creating and Managing Artboards

Design software like Adobe Illustrator offers tools for creating, duplicating, and arranging artboards within a single document. These artboards can have different dimensions, orientations, and purposes, catering to the diverse needs of a project.

2. Enhancing Workflow Efficiency: The Power of Consolidation

Multiple artboards enhance workflow efficiency by consolidating design iterations and variations within one file, eliminating the need for multiple documents and enabling seamless switching between concepts.

Version Management and Comparison

Designers can utilize artboards to manage different versions of a design concept. This feature facilitates easy comparison and evaluation, helping designers make informed decisions and refine their work.

Responsive Design and Multiple Formats

For projects that require designs in various formats (e.g., web and print), multiple artboards are a time-saving solution. Designers can create each format on a separate artboard, ensuring consistency while tailoring designs to different contexts.

3. Organizational Excellence: Creating Order from Chaos

Multiple artboards contribute to organizational excellence by providing a structured canvas for designs, reducing clutter, and ensuring that all elements are easily accessible and organized.

Grouping and Layer Management

Designers can group elements related to specific artboards, maintaining a clear hierarchy. Layers can also be organized to correspond with each artboard, ensuring efficient navigation and editing.

Presentation and Export
Designers can utilize multiple artboards for creating presentation layouts. Once the designs are complete, artboards can be exported as individual files or combined into one document for client reviews or portfolio showcases.

Practical Applications: From UI/UX to Print Design
Multiple artboards have diverse applications across various design disciplines.

User Interface and User Experience (UI/UX) Design
For UI/UX designers, multiple artboards are essential for creating responsive designs that adapt to different screen sizes and orientations. Artboards allow designers to visualize the user experience across various devices.

Print Design and Editorial Layouts
In print design, multiple artboards are invaluable for creating editorial layouts that involve multiple pages or formats. Designers can seamlessly transition between spreads and ensure a cohesive visual language throughout the publication.

Conclusion: Mastering the Symphony of Efficiency
Multiple artboards are the conductor's baton that orchestrates a symphony of efficiency in design. As

designers explore this feature, each artboard becomes a canvas for creativity and organization, contributing to the harmony and coherence of the entire project.

Whether you're creating responsive interfaces, refining print layouts, or exploring diverse design concepts, let multiple artboards be your instrument for efficiency. Embrace their potential, and let them guide your workflow in software like Adobe Illustrator. By consolidating designs, enhancing organization, and simplifying version management, you can transform your design process into a well-structured composition that showcases not only your creative prowess but also your mastery of efficiency in the dynamic world of design.

CREATING PRESENTATIONS, MOCKUPS, AND MULTI-PAGE DOCUMENTS

In the realm of design, the ability to translate concepts into tangible visual narratives is a cornerstone of effective communication. Creating presentations, mockups, and multi-page documents allows designers to tell stories, showcase ideas, and bring designs to life in a dynamic and comprehensive manner. In this article, we delve into the world of crafting presentations, mockups, and multi-page documents, uncovering their potential to engage audiences, streamline design processes, and transform ideas into captivating realities.

1. Presentations as Visual Stories: Communicating Ideas with Impact

Presentations are a powerful medium for conveying ideas, concepts, and information to diverse audiences. They enable designers to combine visuals, text, and multimedia elements to create compelling narratives that resonate with viewers.

Structuring Visual Content

Designers can structure presentations by organizing content into slides that flow logically and cohesively. Each slide becomes a canvas for combining images, graphics, text, and animations to reinforce key points.

Storytelling through Design

Presentations are an opportunity for designers to tell stories through visuals. By using imagery, color, typography, and layout strategically, designers can create presentations that evoke emotions, emphasize messages, and captivate the audience.

2. Mockups: Bringing Designs to Life in Context

Mockups are realistic representations of designs placed within their intended contexts. They offer clients and stakeholders a tangible preview of how the final design will look and function in real-world scenarios.

Realistic Visualization

Designers can create mockups to showcase branding materials, packaging designs, and user interfaces in a realistic context. This visualization helps clients envision the final product and make informed decisions.

Enhancing Communication
Mockups facilitate clear communication between designers and clients. Instead of describing design concepts verbally, designers can provide mockups that allow clients to visualize and provide feedback on specific design elements.

3. Multi-Page Documents: Curating Comprehensive Visual Experiences
Multi-page documents, such as brochures, magazines, and reports, enable designers to curate comprehensive visual experiences that engage readers and convey information effectively.

Layout and Flow
Designers can structure multi-page documents by carefully considering layout, typography, and visual hierarchy. Consistency in design elements across pages ensures a cohesive and engaging reading experience.

Information Presentation
Multi-page documents offer designers the opportunity to present complex information in a digestible format. Through a combination of text, imagery, charts, and infographics, designers can

create documents that educate, inform, and inspire readers.

Practical Applications: From Marketing to Editorial Design

Creating presentations, mockups, and multi-page documents has diverse applications across various design disciplines.

Marketing and Branding

In marketing, designers create presentations to pitch ideas, showcase campaigns, and convey brand messages. Mockups help demonstrate how branding elements will appear in real-world contexts.

Editorial and Publishing

In editorial design, multi-page documents are essential for crafting magazines, brochures, and reports. Each page becomes a canvas for designers to express creativity while delivering content effectively.

Conclusion: Design as Communication and Expression

Creating presentations, mockups, and multi-page documents is a testament to the power of design as a means of communication and expression. As designers explore these mediums, each slide, each mockup, and each page becomes an opportunity to convey messages, evoke emotions, and engage audiences.

Whether you're delivering persuasive presentations, visualizing designs through mockups, or curating comprehensive reading experiences, let these tools be your conduits for creativity and communication. Embrace their potential, and let your designs unfold in software like Adobe Illustrator. By structuring narratives, enhancing realism, and curating visual experiences, you can transform your ideas into captivating visual stories that resonate with viewers, engage readers, and leave a lasting impact in the dynamic world of design.

TECHNIQUES FOR RESPONSIVE AND ADAPTIVE DESIGN USING ARTBOARDS

In the digital landscape, design is no longer confined to fixed dimensions; it must seamlessly adapt to various devices and screen sizes. Responsive and adaptive design are the cornerstones of crafting user-centric experiences that remain visually captivating across platforms. Artboards, the versatile canvases within design software, are the key to achieving this adaptability. In this article, we delve into the world of responsive and adaptive design using artboards, exploring techniques that empower designers to create layouts that fluidly transition from desktops to smartphones, ensuring a harmonious user journey.

1. Responsive vs. Adaptive Design: Crafting Flexibility

Responsive design involves creating layouts that adjust fluidly based on screen size, ensuring optimal viewing experiences. Adaptive design, on the other hand, involves designing specific layouts for predefined breakpoints, catering to various device sizes.

Responsive Design Techniques

Responsive design techniques involve using flexible grids, media queries, and fluid typography to create layouts that adapt smoothly to different screen sizes. Elements reflow and resize, maintaining readability and aesthetics.

Adaptive Design Techniques

Adaptive design relies on predefined breakpoints to design distinct layouts for various screen sizes. Each layout is optimized for a specific range of devices, ensuring the best possible experience for each group.

2. Harnessing Artboards for Responsiveness: Creating Unified Experiences

Artboards are the linchpin of responsive and adaptive design. By utilizing them effectively, designers can create layouts that seamlessly adapt to different devices while maintaining design integrity.

Setting Up Artboards

Design software like Adobe Illustrator enables designers to set up multiple artboards for various breakpoints. These artboards serve as canvases for designing layouts tailored to different device sizes.

Responsive Grid Systems

Designers can create responsive grid systems within artboards to maintain consistent spacing and alignment across different screen sizes. Grids ensure that content adapts harmoniously without compromising the design's integrity.

3. Artboards for Adaptive Breakpoints: Tailoring Experiences

When employing adaptive design, artboards become pivotal for creating layouts that cater to specific device ranges.

Designing for Breakpoints

For each predefined breakpoint, designers create a new artboard optimized for the associated screen size. This approach ensures that the design adapts seamlessly for users on devices within that range.

Testing and Refining

Designers must rigorously test and refine each artboard to ensure that content remains legible and visually appealing on devices within the designated breakpoint range. This iterative process fine-tunes the design for optimal user experiences.

Practical Applications: From Web Design to App Development

Responsive and adaptive design using artboards find application across various design domains.

Web Design

For web designers, responsive design using artboards is vital for creating websites that provide optimal viewing experiences across devices. Artboards enable the creation of fluid layouts that gracefully adapt to different screen sizes.

App Development

In app development, adaptive design using artboards is crucial for ensuring that user interfaces remain user-friendly and visually appealing on various devices. Artboards facilitate the creation of distinct layouts for smartphones, tablets, and desktops.

Conclusion: Designing for Every Device, Every User

Responsive and adaptive design using artboards is an art form that fuses creativity with functionality. As designers explore these techniques, each layout, each breakpoint, and each artboard becomes a piece of the puzzle that contributes to a harmonious user experience across devices.

Whether you're designing websites, apps, or digital interfaces, let responsive and adaptive design using artboards be your guide. Embrace the power they offer, and let them elevate your designs in software like Adobe Illustrator. By creating layouts that fluidly transition between devices, you can transform your designs into versatile masterpieces that engage users, enhance accessibility, and provide a consistent visual journey across the dynamic landscape of digital design.

CHAPTER 9: DATA VISUALIZATION AND INFOGRAPHICS
DESIGNING COMPELLING DATA VISUALIZATIONS WITH CHARTS AND GRAPHS

In the era of information overload, the ability to distill complex data into clear, concise, and visually captivating narratives is a hallmark of effective communication. Data visualizations, achieved through charts and graphs, are powerful tools that enable designers to transform raw data into insights that resonate with audiences. In this article, we delve into the art of designing compelling data visualizations using charts and graphs, uncovering techniques that empower designers to convey information with clarity, impact, and sophistication.

1. The Language of Data: Understanding the Power of Visualizations

Data visualizations are more than just colorful graphics; they're a language that translates raw numbers into stories, trends, and patterns. By visualizing data, designers provide audiences with a visual context that facilitates understanding and facilitates decision-making.

Choosing the Right Visualization

Designers must select the appropriate chart or graph type based on the data they wish to convey. Bar charts, line graphs, pie charts, scatter plots, and more each have their strengths and weaknesses, catering to different data distributions and insights.

Data Simplification and Focus

Effective data visualizations simplify complex information while highlighting key points. Designers must distill data down to the most important elements, ensuring that the visualization maintains a clear focus.

2. Design Principles for Compelling Visualizations: Form and Function

While data visualization is rooted in information, design principles play a crucial role in making visualizations compelling and engaging.

Clarity and Readability

Designers must ensure that data visualizations are clear and legible. Labels, scales, and annotations should be well-placed and easily readable, enabling audiences to quickly grasp the information being presented.

Color and Hierarchy

Color choice and hierarchy guide audiences' attention and convey meaning. Designers can use color to highlight specific data points, trends, or comparisons, while maintaining a harmonious visual balance.

3. Crafting Impactful Data Stories: Enhancing Insights

Data visualizations aren't just about presenting facts; they're about revealing insights and telling stories that resonate with audiences.

Narrative Flow

Designers can create a narrative flow within data visualizations by structuring them in a logical sequence. This allows audiences to follow the data's journey and uncover insights as the story unfolds.

Annotations and Context

Designers can enhance data visualizations by adding annotations that provide context and explanations. These annotations guide audiences through the visualization, ensuring that insights are accurately understood.

Practical Applications: From Business Reports to Infographics

Data visualizations with charts and graphs have diverse applications across various domains.

Business and Analytics

In business, data visualizations are crucial for presenting financial data, performance metrics, and market trends. Visualizations enable stakeholders to make informed decisions based on a clear understanding of the data.

Media and Journalism

In media and journalism, data visualizations bring statistics and research to life, engaging readers and facilitating comprehension of complex issues. Infographics are particularly effective in presenting data-driven stories.

Conclusion: Visuals that Speak Volumes

Data visualization with charts and graphs is an art that marries analytical insight with visual expression. As designers explore these techniques, each chart, each graph, and each visualization becomes a canvas for presenting data as a compelling narrative that informs, enlightens, and empowers.

Whether you're presenting business data, journalistic research, or educational material, let data visualizations with charts and graphs be your tools of choice. Embrace their power, and let them amplify your insights in software like Adobe Illustrator. By crafting clear visuals, following design principles, and telling impactful stories through data, you can transform raw information into dynamic presentations that not only educate but also captivate and inspire, making data a language that speaks volumes in the world of communication.

CRAFTING INFORMATIVE INFOGRAPHICS USING ADVANCED LAYOUT TECHNIQUES

In the digital age, where information is abundant and attention spans are short, the ability to convey complex ideas succinctly and visually is a skill that sets designers apart. Infographics, the artful marriage of design and data, offer a dynamic solution. Through advanced layout techniques, designers can transform data into engaging narratives that captivate audiences and make information memorable. In this article, we delve into the world of crafting informative infographics using advanced layout techniques, exploring strategies that enable designers to create masterpieces that educate, inspire, and resonate.

1. The Power of Infographics: Elevating Communication

Infographics are a visual language that transcends barriers, communicating ideas, statistics, and insights with remarkable efficiency. They offer a multi-dimensional approach to storytelling, enabling designers to present information that appeals to both analytical and creative minds.

Balancing Form and Function

Effective infographics strike a balance between aesthetics and functionality. While design elements should captivate, they must also serve the purpose of conveying information clearly and cohesively.

Choosing the Right Visual Hierarchy
Designers must prioritize information within infographics by creating a visual hierarchy. This ensures that the most important data is immediately noticeable, guiding audiences through the narrative.

2. Advanced Layout Techniques: Navigating Complexity
Creating informative infographics requires more than just arranging elements; it demands mastery of advanced layout techniques that enable the seamless integration of design and data.

Data Visualization Techniques
Designers can utilize various data visualization techniques, such as bar charts, line graphs, and pie charts, to present statistical information in an easily digestible format. These techniques offer clarity while maintaining a visually engaging presentation.

Whitespace and Visual Flow
Whitespace is a powerful tool for directing the viewer's attention and enhancing visual flow. Designers can strategically use whitespace to separate sections, guide the eye, and prevent information overload.

3. Storytelling through Composition: Weaving the Narrative
An effective infographic is not a mere collection of data points; it's a narrative that takes the audience on

a journey. Designers must leverage composition techniques to create a cohesive and compelling story.

Sequential Storytelling
Sequential storytelling involves guiding the audience through the infographic in a logical sequence. This technique uses visual cues to lead the viewer from one piece of information to the next, creating a fluid narrative.

Iconography and Illustration
Icons and illustrations can simplify complex concepts, making information more accessible. Designers can create custom icons or use existing ones to enhance visual appeal and aid comprehension.

Practical Applications: From Education to Marketing
Informative infographics with advanced layout techniques find application across diverse fields.

Educational Material
In education, infographics are valuable tools for presenting academic concepts, historical timelines, and scientific processes. The combination of visuals and text aids understanding and retention.

Marketing and Communication
In marketing, infographics serve as attention-grabbing tools for presenting product features, industry trends, and brand narratives. Compelling visuals help convey messages effectively in a crowded digital landscape.

Conclusion: Infographics that Inspire Insight

Creating informative infographics with advanced layout techniques is a journey that transforms data into insight. As designers explore these techniques, each layout, each composition, and each visual element becomes a stroke of creativity that enriches the narrative.

Whether you're crafting educational materials, marketing content, or data-driven stories, let informative infographics be your medium. Embrace the techniques they offer, and let them empower your creativity in software like Adobe Illustrator. By combining data visualization, storytelling composition, and advanced layout techniques, you can transform information into interactive journeys that educate, inspire, and leave a lasting impact in the dynamic realm of visual communication.

INCORPORATING INTERACTIVITY FOR DIGITAL PUBLICATIONS

In the ever-evolving landscape of digital content consumption, engagement is key. Static content no longer suffices; audiences crave immersive experiences that allow them to participate, explore, and connect. Incorporating interactivity into digital publications offers a transformative solution. By infusing dynamic elements, animations, and multimedia, designers can create publications that captivate, educate, and inspire in ways that traditional mediums cannot. In this article, we delve into the realm of incorporating interactivity for digital publications, uncovering techniques that empower designers to create engaging masterpieces that redefine how audiences interact with content.

1. The Age of Interaction: Understanding the Impact of Interactive Content

Interactive content transcends passive consumption, inviting audiences to become active participants in the narrative. It fosters engagement, enriches understanding, and heightens emotional connection, transforming the reading experience into a dynamic journey.

Interactive Elements and their Benefits

Incorporating interactive elements like buttons, animations, and multimedia enhances the overall appeal of digital publications. These elements serve as visual cues that guide readers' attention, evoke emotions, and encourage exploration.

Engagement and Exploration

Interactive publications encourage readers to explore content at their own pace. They can click, swipe, and interact with various elements, uncovering additional information, visuals, and surprises along the way.

2. Crafting Interactive Experiences: Techniques for Engagement

Creating interactive digital publications requires a blend of design finesse, technical prowess, and storytelling acumen. Designers must wield various tools and techniques to craft experiences that seamlessly integrate interactivity.

Animation and Transitions
Animations lend a dynamic quality to digital publications. Smooth transitions, subtle animations, and interactive effects create a sense of continuity and flow, enhancing the overall experience.

Multimedia Integration
Incorporating multimedia elements such as videos, audio clips, and interactive graphics elevates engagement. Designers can create multimedia hotspots that offer additional insights, explanations, or emotional resonance.

3. User Experience Design: Navigating the Interactive Landscape
User experience (UX) design is paramount in interactive digital publications. Designers must prioritize intuitive navigation, responsive layouts, and seamless interactions to ensure a user-friendly and enjoyable experience.

Responsive Design
Interactive content should adapt flawlessly to various screen sizes and orientations. Responsive design ensures that the interactive elements function seamlessly on desktops, tablets, and smartphones.

User-Centered Navigation

User-centered navigation is crucial. Designers must consider user behavior and preferences when placing interactive elements and ensuring that they enhance, rather than hinder, the reading experience.

Practical Applications: From eBooks to Digital Magazines

Incorporating interactivity into digital publications has diverse applications across various industries.

eBooks and Learning Materials

For educational purposes, interactive eBooks offer enriched learning experiences. Quizzes, interactive diagrams, and multimedia can enhance understanding and engagement for learners.

Digital Magazines and Catalogs

In digital publishing, interactive magazines and catalogs redefine how content is presented. Videos, animations, and interactive galleries allow readers to delve deeper into topics and products.

Conclusion: Redefining Engagement through Interaction

Incorporating interactivity into digital publications is an art that unites creativity and technology. As designers explore these techniques, each animation, each multimedia integration, and each interactive element becomes a conduit for engagement and connection.

Whether you're crafting educational materials, marketing content, or digital stories, let interactivity be your catalyst for immersive experiences. Embrace the techniques it offers, and let them redefine your creativity in software like Adobe InDesign. By infusing animations, multimedia, and user-centric design principles, you can transform digital publications into captivating journeys that educate, entertain, and foster lasting connections in the dynamic realm of digital storytelling.

CHAPTER 10: AUTOMATION AND WORKFLOW ENHANCEMENTS
STREAMLINING REPETITIVE TASKS WITH ACTIONS AND BATCH PROCESSING

In the world of design, time is a valuable resource, and efficiency is the key to success. Repetitive tasks, although necessary, can be a drain on creativity and productivity. Enter Actions and Batch Processing, the dynamic duo that empowers designers to transform mundane tasks into automated workflows. In this article, we delve into the realm of streamlining repetitive tasks with Actions and Batch Processing, exploring techniques that allow designers to reclaim their time, boost productivity, and focus on what truly matters—creative innovation.

1. The Quest for Efficiency: Understanding the Power of Automation

Repetitive tasks, such as resizing images, applying filters, and renaming files, can consume precious hours that could be better spent on more creative endeavors. Automation through Actions and Batch Processing offers a solution that not only saves time but also enhances consistency and accuracy.

Actions: Recorded Brilliance

Actions are sequences of recorded steps in design software that can be replayed on demand. By recording and executing repetitive tasks, designers create a digital assistant that performs actions with precision.

Batch Processing: Empowering Mass Transformation
Batch Processing extends the power of Actions to multiple files simultaneously. Designers can apply the same recorded sequence of steps to numerous files, transforming entire folders of content with a single command.

2. Crafting Automated Workflows: Mastering the Art of Efficiency
Creating efficient workflows through Actions and Batch Processing involves careful planning, execution, and customization. Designers must strategize to ensure that automation enhances their work without sacrificing quality.

Recording Custom Actions
Designers can record custom Actions for tasks like resizing images, applying filters, or adding watermarks. Custom Actions allow for personalization and fine-tuning, ensuring that automation aligns with specific project requirements.

Batch Processing Multiple Files
Batch Processing involves selecting a group of files and applying a recorded Action to all of them. Designers can choose various options, such as output file format, location, and naming conventions, to tailor the process to their needs.

3. Tailoring Automation for Creative Needs: Flexibility and Control

While automation is a powerful ally, it's essential to strike a balance between automation and creative control. Designers must customize Actions and Batch Processing to ensure that their work maintains its unique touch.

Action Customization

Customizing Actions allows designers to edit recorded steps and make adjustments to suit different projects. This flexibility ensures that automation serves as a tool for enhancing, not replacing, creativity.

Quality Assurance

Even with automation, designers must perform quality checks to ensure that the results meet their standards. Batch Processing may require adjustments for specific files, sizes, or content variations.

Practical Applications: From Image Editing to Graphic Creation

Actions and Batch Processing have diverse applications across various design disciplines.

Image Editing

In image editing, Actions can be used to automate tasks like color correction, retouching, and resizing for different platforms. Batch Processing streamlines the process of preparing multiple images for various uses.

Graphic Creation
For graphic designers, Actions and Batch Processing can assist in creating repetitive elements such as logos, icons, and patterns. These tools ensure consistency while freeing up time for more intricate design work.

Conclusion: Unleashing Creativity through Efficiency
Streamlining repetitive tasks with Actions and Batch Processing is a revelation that empowers designers to focus on creativity. As designers explore these techniques, each recorded Action, each batch process, and each automated workflow becomes a testament to the synergy between innovation and efficiency.

Whether you're working with images, graphics, or multimedia, let Actions and Batch Processing be your instruments of efficiency. Embrace their potential, and let them elevate your productivity in software like Adobe Photoshop. By automating tasks, customizing actions, and finding the perfect balance between automation and creative control, you can transform your workflow into a symphony of streamlined efficiency that amplifies your creative brilliance in the dynamic world of design.

UTILIZING SCRIPTS AND PLUG-INS FOR EXTENDED FUNCTIONALITY

In the realm of design, the quest for innovation is unceasing. However, the demands of complex tasks and intricate workflows can often hinder creative expression. Enter scripts and plug-ins, the dynamic duo that extends the capabilities of design software, empowering designers to achieve feats that were once deemed daunting. In this article, we delve into the world of utilizing scripts and plug-ins for extended functionality, exploring techniques that allow designers to break free from limitations, streamline workflows, and push the boundaries of creative exploration.

1. Expanding Horizons: Understanding the Power of Scripts and Plug-ins

Scripts and plug-ins are tools that enhance the functionality of design software by introducing automation, customization, and features beyond the native capabilities. They bridge the gap between creative vision and technical execution, unlocking new possibilities for designers.

Scripts: Automating Magic

Scripts are code snippets that automate specific tasks or actions within design software. They can range from simple tasks like renaming layers to complex operations like generating intricate patterns.

Plug-ins: Enriching the Toolbox

Plug-ins are external modules that integrate with design software to introduce new features, effects, or functionalities. They expand the software's capabilities without requiring users to be proficient in coding.

2. Crafting Efficiency through Scripts: Automating Repetitive Tasks

Scripts empower designers to automate repetitive tasks, allowing them to focus on creative aspects without being bogged down by mundane operations.

Custom Script Development

Designers can develop custom scripts tailored to their specific needs. Whether it's batch processing images, generating placeholder content, or applying intricate effects, custom scripts save time and ensure consistency.

Community-Shared Scripts

Design communities often share scripts that address common pain points. Designers can leverage these resources to quickly integrate automation into their workflow and discover new ways to work efficiently.

3. Expanding Horizons with Plug-ins: Enriching the Creative Arsenal

Plug-ins open doors to a world of possibilities by introducing features that might not be available natively in design software.

Plug-ins for Specialized Effects

Designers can use plug-ins to access advanced effects and techniques that might otherwise require extensive manual work. These plug-ins enhance the visual appeal of designs and add a unique touch.

Productivity-Boosting Plug-ins

Many plug-ins are designed to streamline workflows, providing tools for organizing layers, generating assets, and managing color palettes. These plug-ins optimize the design process and increase productivity.

Practical Applications: From Graphic Design to Animation

Utilizing scripts and plug-ins for extended functionality has applications across various design domains.

Graphic Design

In graphic design, scripts and plug-ins can assist in tasks like creating custom typography, applying filters, and generating complex patterns. They allow designers to push the boundaries of visual creativity.

Animation and Motion Graphics

For animators and motion graphic artists, scripts and plug-ins can automate repetitive animation sequences, generate particle effects, and enhance visual dynamics. They elevate animation complexity while saving time.

Conclusion: Design Beyond Limits

Utilizing scripts and plug-ins for extended functionality is an invitation to explore design beyond traditional boundaries. As designers explore these techniques, each script, each plug-in, and each new feature becomes a catalyst for innovation and efficiency.

Whether you're a graphic designer, an animator, or an illustrator, let scripts and plug-ins be your tools of extended creativity. Embrace their potential, and let them amplify your capabilities in software like Adobe Creative Cloud. By automating tasks, introducing specialized effects, and accessing advanced features, you can transform your design practice into a realm of limitless possibilities, where every idea, no matter how complex, can be executed with finesse and precision.

INTEGRATING ILLUSTRATOR WITH OTHER ADOBE CREATIVE CLOUD APPLICATIONS

In the realm of design, creativity knows no bounds. However, the true magic emerges when diverse tools seamlessly collaborate, transforming individual efforts into harmonious masterpieces. Integrating Adobe Illustrator with other Creative Cloud applications is the bridge that connects design disciplines, enabling designers to explore uncharted territories and craft multidimensional creations. In this article, we delve into the world of integrating

Illustrator with other Adobe Creative Cloud applications, exploring techniques that empower designers to transcend boundaries, foster collaboration, and bring their artistic visions to life with unmatched synergy.

1. The Art of Collaboration: Understanding the Power of Integration

Design is a multifaceted endeavor that often requires the collective contributions of various disciplines. Integrating Illustrator with other Creative Cloud applications facilitates collaboration, enabling designers, photographers, animators, and more to work together seamlessly.

Unified Workspace with Creative Cloud Libraries

Creative Cloud Libraries serve as centralized repositories for assets such as colors, graphics, and typography. By integrating Illustrator with libraries, designers ensure consistency across projects and streamline asset sharing among Creative Cloud applications.

Collaborative Workflows

Integrating Illustrator with applications like Adobe Photoshop, InDesign, and After Effects allows for a collaborative workflow where different aspects of a project can be tackled by experts in their respective fields. For instance, a graphic designer can create vector elements in Illustrator, which a motion graphics artist can then animate in After Effects.

2. Bridging Design and Photography: Illustrator and Photoshop Integration

The integration between Adobe Illustrator and Photoshop bridges the gap between vector and raster design, offering a dynamic toolkit that combines the strengths of both applications.

Smart Objects and Vector Masking

Designers can bring vector artwork from Illustrator into Photoshop as Smart Objects. This retains the scalability of vectors while allowing designers to apply non-destructive raster effects and masking techniques.

Seamless Texture Creation

By combining Illustrator's vector capabilities with Photoshop's texturing tools, designers can create intricate textures that can be applied to 3D models, digital paintings, and more.

3. Transcending Print and Digital: Illustrator and InDesign Integration

The relationship between Adobe Illustrator and InDesign is pivotal for projects that involve both print and digital mediums, such as magazines, brochures, and interactive PDFs.

Efficient Layouts

Designers can create vector graphics and illustrations in Illustrator and seamlessly import them into

InDesign layouts. This ensures that designs maintain crisp quality across various sizes and resolutions.

Interactive Elements
Integrating Illustrator-created graphics with InDesign layouts allows designers to incorporate interactive elements, such as buttons, hyperlinks, and multimedia, into digital publications.

Practical Applications: From Branding to Motion Graphics
Integrating Illustrator with other Adobe Creative Cloud applications finds applications across diverse design disciplines.

Branding and Identity Design
For brand designers, integrating Illustrator with Photoshop and InDesign allows for a comprehensive approach. Logos and graphics can be created in Illustrator, then incorporated into mockups and brand guidelines in Photoshop and InDesign.

Motion Graphics and Animation
Motion graphic artists can create vector graphics in Illustrator and then animate them in After Effects. The integration enables the seamless transfer of assets, streamlining the motion design process.

Conclusion: The Creative Symphony
Integrating Adobe Illustrator with other Creative Cloud applications transforms design into a symphony

of collaboration, creativity, and functionality. As designers explore these techniques, each integration, each collaborative project, and each creative endeavor becomes a testament to the potential of unified creativity.

Whether you're a graphic designer, an animator, or a multimedia artist, let the integration of Illustrator with other Creative Cloud applications be your creative symphony. Embrace the power they offer, and let them amplify your artistic vision. By collaborating, bridging mediums, and transcending traditional boundaries, you can transform your design practice into a harmonious blend of disciplines, where innovation is boundless, and the possibilities are limited only by your imagination.

CHAPTER 11: EXPORTING AND COLLABORATION CHOOSING THE RIGHT FILE FORMATS FOR DIFFERENT PURPOSES

In the digital realm, the right file format can make or break a design's impact and functionality. Choosing the appropriate file format is an art that requires an understanding of the nuances of each format's capabilities, strengths, and weaknesses. In this article, we delve into the world of file formats, exploring the intricacies of choosing the right format for different design purposes. By mastering the art of format selection, designers can ensure that their creations shine in the best light, whether they're on the web, in print, or in motion.

1. The Language of Formats: Grasping the Significance

File formats are more than just extensions; they're languages that dictate how digital content is displayed, stored, and transmitted. Different formats serve distinct purposes, and understanding their characteristics is pivotal for effective design.

Raster vs. Vector Formats

Raster formats, such as JPEG and PNG, store images as grids of pixels. They're ideal for photographs and complex visuals. Vector formats, like SVG and AI, store images as mathematical equations. They're suitable for logos, icons, and graphics that require scalability.

Lossy vs. Lossless Compression

Some formats, like JPEG, use lossy compression, sacrificing some image quality for smaller file sizes. Others, like PNG and TIFF, employ lossless compression, preserving image quality at the cost of larger file sizes.

2. Tailoring Formats to Different Design Needs: A Comprehensive Guide

Choosing the right file format involves aligning the format's strengths with the design's intended purpose, be it web, print, animation, or something else entirely.

Web Design and Graphics

For web design and online graphics, formats like JPEG and PNG are popular choices. JPEG is ideal for photographs, while PNG supports transparent backgrounds and crisp graphics.

Print Design and Typography

Print design requires high-resolution formats for sharp output. TIFF and PDF are favored for print-ready materials, as they support lossless compression and embed fonts.

Motion Graphics and Animation

In motion graphics and animation, formats like GIF, APNG, and MP4 come into play. GIF is suitable for simple animations, while APNG and MP4 offer higher quality and smoother motion.

3. Format Conversion and Adaptation: Flexibility in Action

Converting and adapting formats allows designers to repurpose content for various platforms without compromising quality.

Converting Raster to Vector

Designers can convert raster images to vector format using tools like Adobe Illustrator's Image Trace feature. This enables scalability and editing flexibility for images that were initially pixel-based.

Exporting for Different Devices

Designers should optimize content for different devices by considering factors like screen size and resolution. Exporting content in multiple formats ensures that the design remains visually appealing across various platforms.

Practical Applications: From Social Media to Video Editing

Choosing the right file formats for different purposes spans various design domains.

Social Media Graphics

For social media graphics, formats like JPEG and PNG are commonly used. JPEG offers high-quality visuals, while PNG preserves transparent backgrounds and sharp edges.

Video Editing and Effects

In video editing, formats like MOV and AVI are suitable for maintaining video quality during editing. Exporting final videos in formats like MP4 ensures compatibility and streaming efficiency.

Conclusion: A Format Odyssey

Choosing the right file formats for different design purposes is a journey that requires an understanding of each format's nuances. As designers explore these techniques, each format selection, each conversion, and each adaptation becomes a testament to the adaptability and versatility of design.

Whether you're designing for the web, print, animation, or multimedia, let the choice of file format be your guide. Embrace the diversity they offer, and let them amplify your creations. By aligning strengths with needs, converting formats with finesse, and optimizing content for various devices, you can transform your design practice into a realm of flexibility, where your artistic vision thrives regardless of the medium, platform, or purpose.

PREPARING DESIGNS FOR PRINT, WEB, AND MOBILE

In the modern design landscape, versatility is the cornerstone of success. Creating a captivating design is only the first step; ensuring its seamless adaptation across different mediums is where the real art lies. Preparing designs for print, web, and mobile demands an understanding of the unique requirements, constraints, and nuances of each platform. In this article, we delve into the world of design adaptability, exploring techniques that empower designers to navigate the intricacies of preparing their creations for print, web, and mobile. By mastering the art of versatile preparation, designers can ensure that their work shines across all corners of the digital and physical realm.

1. The Triad of Adaptation: Recognizing the Diversity

Print, web, and mobile are distinct landscapes, each with its own set of demands and dimensions. Preparing designs for these mediums requires a strategic approach that accounts for their unique attributes.

Print: Precision and Resolution

Print demands high-resolution files with rich colors to ensure crisp output. Understanding color modes (CMYK) and using vector formats like PDF or AI are essential for accurate reproduction.

Web: Responsive and Dynamic

Web design must consider responsive layouts that adapt to various screen sizes. Raster formats like JPEG and PNG are commonly used, and optimizing images for web loading speed is crucial.

Mobile: Scalability and Interaction

Mobile design centers around scalability and touch interaction. Vector formats like SVG are beneficial for maintaining sharpness, and responsive design principles ensure seamless experiences on different devices.

2. Crafting Versatile Assets: Techniques for Each Medium

Designers must adopt different strategies for each medium, ensuring that their artwork shines regardless of the platform it's viewed on.

Print-Ready Design

For print, designers must set up their artwork with proper bleeds, trim marks, and safe zones to account for the cutting and printing process. Exporting in high-resolution formats like PDF/X ensures the design's fidelity.

Responsive Web Layouts

In web design, using responsive frameworks like Bootstrap and employing CSS media queries allows designers to create layouts that adapt fluidly to various screen sizes. Designers must also optimize images for web performance using tools like image compression and lazy loading.

Mobile-Friendly Elements

Mobile design requires larger tap targets, simplified navigation, and legible typography. Designers must create interfaces that consider touch gestures and accommodate the smaller screens of smartphones and tablets.

3. Consistency and Brand Identity: Across All Platforms
Maintaining brand consistency across print, web, and mobile is pivotal. Designers must ensure that the visual elements, colors, and typography align with the brand's identity, regardless of the medium.

Color Consistency
Designers must ensure that color palettes remain consistent across print and digital platforms. Converting colors from RGB to CMYK for print, and vice versa for web and mobile, prevents color shifts.

Typography Harmony
Typography should be legible and maintain consistent sizing across mediums. Designers must choose fonts that are available and render well on both screens and in print.

Practical Applications: From Brochures to Mobile Apps
Preparing designs for print, web, and mobile has applications across various design domains.

Printed Collateral

For print materials like brochures, business cards, and posters, designers must ensure that the design elements are set up correctly for printing and maintain a professional appearance.

Web and User Interface Design

In web and UI design, designers must create layouts that are responsive and visually appealing across different devices and screen sizes, ensuring seamless experiences for users.

Conclusion: The Seamless Journey

Preparing designs for print, web, and mobile is a journey that showcases a designer's adaptability and versatility. As designers explore these techniques, each print-ready setup, each responsive layout, and each mobile-friendly element becomes a testament to the designer's prowess in navigating diverse mediums.

Whether you're crafting print materials, web layouts, or mobile interfaces, let the art of adaptation be your guiding light. Embrace the versatility that each medium demands, and let them amplify your creative expression. By mastering print specifications, responsive design, and mobile-friendly principles, you can transform your design practice into a realm where your creations flourish seamlessly, resonating across the canvas of print, the virtual realm of the web, and the palm of the mobile screen.

COLLABORATIVE WORKFLOWS USING CLOUD-BASED SERVICES AND SHARED LIBRARIES

In the dynamic landscape of design, collaboration is the cornerstone of innovation. The ability to seamlessly connect, share, and work together in real-time has redefined the way creative projects come to life. Cloud-based services and shared libraries have emerged as powerful catalysts for collaborative workflows, enabling designers to transcend geographical barriers, amplify efficiency, and foster a creative synergy that elevates projects to new heights. In this article, we delve into the realm of collaborative design, exploring the intricate dance of cloud-based services and shared libraries that revolutionize the way designers work together, bridging gaps, and crafting masterpieces that are truly collective achievements.

1. The Collaboration Revolution: Understanding the Power of the Cloud

Cloud-based services have revolutionized the concept of teamwork, providing a virtual canvas where designers can collectively shape their visions.

Centralized Storage and Accessibility

Cloud-based platforms like Adobe Creative Cloud offer centralized storage that hosts project files and assets. This accessibility means that collaborators can work from anywhere with an internet connection.

Real-Time Collaboration

Cloud-based services enable real-time collaboration, where multiple team members can simultaneously edit and view the same document. This streamlines communication and minimizes version control issues.

2. Shared Libraries: A Symphony of Creativity

Shared libraries take collaboration a step further by allowing designers to share assets, styles, and resources across projects and collaborators.

Centralized Asset Management

Shared libraries provide a central repository for assets like logos, icons, and color palettes. Designers can access and utilize these elements across multiple projects, ensuring consistency.

Consistency Across Projects

By using shared libraries, collaborators can maintain visual consistency across different projects, regardless of who's working on them. This helps reinforce brand identity and design standards.

3. Collaborative Workflow in Action: Techniques for Success

Collaborative workflows through cloud-based services and shared libraries require strategic planning and thoughtful execution to ensure a smooth and effective process.

Effective Folder and File Organization

Designers should establish clear folder structures and naming conventions within cloud storage platforms. This ensures that collaborators can quickly locate files and understand their purpose.

Version History and Collaboration Modes

Most cloud-based platforms offer version history features that track changes and allow collaborators to revert to previous versions. Additionally, collaboration modes enable specific access and editing permissions.

Practical Applications: From Graphic Design to Video Production

Collaborative workflows using cloud-based services and shared libraries are applicable across various design domains.

Graphic Design

For graphic designers, collaborative workflows enable teams to work together on branding projects, marketing collateral, and digital assets, ensuring a cohesive visual identity.

Video Production and Editing

In video production, cloud-based platforms facilitate collaboration among editors, animators, and sound designers. Shared libraries help maintain consistent visual elements and soundtracks.

Conclusion: The Nexus of Creativity
Collaborative workflows driven by cloud-based services and shared libraries redefine the boundaries of design. As designers explore these techniques, each collaborative project, each shared asset, and each real-time edit becomes a testament to the creative nexus that transcends time and space.

Whether you're designing logos, creating marketing campaigns, or producing multimedia content, let collaborative workflows be your creative symphony. Embrace the connectivity they offer, and let them amplify your collective potential. By leveraging cloud-based platforms, shared libraries, and effective collaboration strategies, you can transform your design practice into a realm where collaboration is seamless, innovation flourishes, and the results speak volumes of the harmonious symphony of creativity.

CONCLUSION
RECAP OF KEY TAKEAWAYS FROM THE BOOK

In the journey of design excellence, knowledge is the compass that guides us. As we explored the intricacies of advanced Illustrator usage, integrated interactive elements, harnessed automation, and navigated the intricacies of various platforms, a wealth of insights has emerged. In this recap, we distill the key takeaways from the exploration of Adobe Illustrator's potential and its integration into the broader world of design. These takeaways serve as guiding stars, illuminating the path to design brilliance.

1. Advanced Illustrator Mastery: Elevating Creativity
The journey from beginner to advanced user in Illustrator is marked by a shift in mindset. Embrace the tools, techniques, and principles that empower intricate vector artwork, dynamic typography, and captivating compositions. Transition from mere creation to mastery, allowing your creative expression to flourish.

2. Seamless Integration and Versatility
In the interconnected realm of design, the integration of Adobe Illustrator with other Creative Cloud applications unveils new horizons. Seamlessly move between Illustrator, Photoshop, InDesign, and beyond, harnessing each application's unique strengths to craft versatile and impactful designs.

3. Interaction Unleashed: Interactivity for Engagement
Elevate digital publications from static to dynamic by incorporating interactivity. Engage audiences through animations, multimedia, and responsive elements. By embracing interactivity, you transform content consumption into immersive exploration, fostering deeper connections and understanding.

4. Automation and Streamlining: Actions and Batch Processing
Efficiency is the catalyst of creativity. Embrace the power of automation through Actions and Batch Processing. Free yourself from repetitive tasks and

focus on innovation by scripting routines and streamlining workflows, allowing your creative brilliance to shine through.

5. Formats: Tailoring for Diverse Mediums
In the world of digital and print, the right file format is the key to impactful design. Choose formats wisely based on their characteristics and strengths. Ensure designs adapt seamlessly to print, web, and mobile platforms, capturing attention and delivering consistent experiences.

6. Collaboration and Adaptation: Cloud and Libraries
The era of solitary creation is over. Cloud-based services and shared libraries redefine collaboration. Work harmoniously across geographical boundaries, share assets effortlessly, and maintain brand consistency. Harness the power of real-time collaboration and versatile asset sharing to amplify creativity.

7. Unified Preparation: Print, Web, and Mobile
Prepare designs for diverse platforms with finesse. Understand the nuances of print, web, and mobile requirements. Craft responsive layouts, optimize images, and ensure scalability, creating designs that thrive across all mediums, resonating with audiences everywhere.

8. From Individual Endeavors to Collective Achievements

Design is not just about individual brilliance; it's about collective achievements. Collaborate, integrate, and innovate. Unite cloud-based services, shared libraries, and interactive elements to create designs that transcend boundaries and redefine the possibilities of creativity.

In Conclusion: The Canvas of Design Excellence

As we recap these key takeaways, we realize that design brilliance is not just about mastering software; it's about embracing the principles, strategies, and techniques that amplify creativity. From mastering Illustrator's advanced tools to integrating diverse platforms, from harnessing automation to crafting adaptable designs, each takeaway forms a brushstroke on the canvas of design excellence. Embrace these insights, let them guide your creative journey, and see how each concept, each integration, and each strategy collectively transform your designs from ordinary to extraordinary.

ENCOURAGEMENT TO CONTİNUE EXPLORİNG AND PUSHİNG THE BOUNDARİES

In the realm of design, the journey is boundless, and the creative spirit knows no bounds. As you've delved into the depths of advanced Illustrator techniques, collaborated across platforms, and crafted designs that captivate, a universe of possibilities has unveiled itself. Now, as you stand at the threshold of this ever-expanding realm, we extend a fervent encouragement to continue exploring, innovating, and pushing the boundaries of your creative expression.

1. Embrace the Uncharted Territory
Innovation flourishes in the unknown. As you navigate through your design journey, remember that every unexplored corner holds the potential for inspiration. Be unafraid to venture into uncharted territories, experiment with new techniques, and redefine what's possible in the world of design.

2. Cultivate a Creative Fearlessness
Creativity thrives when fear takes a back seat. Don't let the fear of failure or the unknown stifle your imagination. Embrace a creative fearlessness that empowers you to take risks, make bold choices, and transform setbacks into stepping stones toward greater innovation.

3. Continuous Learning and Growth
The design landscape is in perpetual motion, shaped by evolving trends and technologies. Keep the fire of learning burning bright. Cultivate a hunger for knowledge that drives you to seek out new skills, stay updated with industry trends, and constantly evolve as a designer.

4. The Power of Collaboration

Collaboration is the conduit for groundbreaking ideas. Embrace the opportunity to work with fellow creatives, share insights, and synergize diverse perspectives. The collision of minds sparks innovation, propelling you beyond your individual capabilities.

5. From Imitation to Innovation

While learning from others is a cornerstone of growth, remember that true innovation requires forging your path. Strive to move beyond imitation and tap into your unique creative voice. Let your designs reflect your perspective, experiences, and passions.

6. Embrace Design Thinking

Design isn't just about aesthetics; it's about solving problems and enhancing experiences. Embrace the principles of design thinking, approaching challenges with empathy, curiosity, and a commitment to finding solutions that resonate deeply with users.

7. Let Curiosity Be Your Guide

Curiosity is the compass that leads to discovery. Cultivate a curious mindset that propels you to ask questions, explore new techniques, and unravel the mysteries of design. Let your curiosity be the force that propels your creativity forward.

8. Celebrate Each Milestone

The journey of a designer is a series of milestones that mark your progress. Celebrate each achievement, no matter how small. Acknowledge your growth, from mastering a new tool to completing a challenging project, and let these successes fuel your passion.

9. Keep Dreaming and Designing
Dreams fuel design, and design fuels dreams. As you push the boundaries, remember that the sky's the limit. Keep dreaming big, envisioning extraordinary possibilities, and translating those visions into designs that transcend the ordinary.

In Conclusion: The Ever-Evolving Odyssey
As you continue your design odyssey, remember that the path is ever-evolving. The knowledge you've gained, the skills you've honed, and the inspiration you've cultivated are the foundation of your journey. Keep pushing the boundaries, keep seeking new horizons, and keep breathing life into your artistic vision. Your designs are more than compositions; they're testaments to your creativity, resilience, and the unyielding passion that propels you forward in the world of design. Embrace the infinite horizon that stretches before you, for the canvas of your creativity is vast, and the potential for brilliance is limitless.

FINAL THOUGHTS ON ACHIEVING BRILLIANCE IN ILLUSTRATOR'S ADVANCED USAGE

As we draw the curtain on this exploration of Adobe Illustrator's advanced capabilities, we find ourselves at the intersection of knowledge and creativity, armed with a wealth of insights and techniques that empower us to craft designs that resonate deeply. The journey from novice to virtuoso in Illustrator is marked by dedication, curiosity, and an unquenchable thirst for pushing the boundaries. In these final thoughts, we reflect on the essence of achieving brilliance in Illustrator's advanced usage, underscoring the fusion of skill, innovation, and passion that sets the stage for transformative design experiences.

1. The Convergence of Skill and Vision

Mastery in advanced Illustrator usage is not solely about mastering tools; it's about honing the craft of transforming visions into reality. As you've delved into intricate drawing tools, harnessed the power of shapes, and navigated the world of typography, you've realized that technical skill becomes the conduit for your creative vision.

2. The Dance of Technique and Innovation

Techniques are the threads that weave the tapestry of innovation. While techniques are essential, true brilliance emerges when you innovate within those techniques. Merge your technical prowess with bold experimentation, unearthing novel ways to use familiar tools and creating designs that stand out in a sea of conformity.

3. The Symphony of Efficiency and Creativity

Efficiency liberates creativity. Through the art of automation, shared libraries, and collaborative workflows, you've learned that streamlining repetitive tasks is the cornerstone of unleashing your creative potential. The more efficiently you work, the more time you have to explore, ideate, and refine your designs.

4. The Elevation of Adaptability

A brilliant designer is one who can navigate the diverse terrain of design mediums. Your journey has led you to comprehend the intricacies of print, web, and mobile design, showcasing adaptability as a key to design excellence. Being able to tailor your creations to different contexts is the hallmark of a true design virtuoso.

5. The Nexus of Collaboration and Expression

Brilliance thrives in collaboration. As you've integrated Illustrator into the broader ecosystem of Adobe Creative Cloud, the ability to seamlessly collaborate and share assets has unlocked a realm of collective innovation. Collaborative workflows and shared libraries have underscored the symbiotic relationship between individual expression and collective achievement.

6. The Ripple Effect of Inspiration

Your journey in mastering advanced Illustrator usage is not just personal; it's a catalyst for inspiring others.

Every design, every technique, and every insight you share has the potential to ignite sparks of creativity in fellow designers. Embrace your role as a source of inspiration, and let your brilliance serve as a beacon for others to follow.

In Conclusion: An Ongoing Odyssey
As we conclude this voyage through advanced Illustrator usage, remember that the pursuit of brilliance is not a destination; it's an ongoing odyssey. The techniques you've honed, the insights you've gained, and the creative spark you've cultivated are the compasses that guide you through the evolving landscape of design. Continue to experiment, innovate, and evolve. Let each design be a canvas for your imagination, a testament to your growth, and an invitation to push the boundaries of what's possible.

Your journey in mastering advanced Illustrator usage is a testament to your dedication, curiosity, and the unyielding pursuit of design excellence. As you continue to unravel the layers of Illustrator's potential and craft designs that resonate with depth, know that the brilliance you've achieved is just a stepping stone to the infinite possibilities that lie ahead. Your creativity is boundless, your potential is limitless, and your impact on the world of design is immeasurable.

APPENDIX:
RESOURCES FOR FURTHER LEARNING AND EXPLORATION

As the voyage through the realm of design continues, the thirst for knowledge remains unquenched. The landscape of design is ever-evolving, and the path to mastery is one of perpetual learning and exploration. In this final chapter, we present a treasure trove of resources that will propel you further along the journey of design brilliance. From online courses to communities, tools, and sources of inspiration, these resources will serve as your guiding stars, illuminating the path to continuous growth and creative excellence.

1. Online Learning Platforms

Udemy: Explore a plethora of courses on design, from Illustrator mastery to advanced typography techniques. Udemy offers a vast collection of tutorials taught by industry experts.

Coursera: Discover courses from renowned universities and institutions worldwide. Their design-related courses cover topics ranging from graphic design fundamentals to interactive web design.

LinkedIn Learning (formerly Lynda.com): Dive deep into a variety of design topics with comprehensive video tutorials and courses. LinkedIn Learning offers a broad spectrum of design-related content.

Skillshare: Immerse yourself in a diverse range of design classes, taught by professionals from various fields. From Illustrator tricks to graphic design principles, Skillshare offers a platform for both beginners and seasoned designers.

2. Communities and Forums

Behance: Join a global community of creatives, share your work, and gain inspiration from fellow designers. Behance is a hub for discovering innovative design projects and collaborating with like-minded individuals.

Dribbble: Engage with a community of designers, showcasing your work and exploring a wide array of design styles. Dribbble provides a platform for sharing small design snippets and receiving constructive feedback.

Adobe Community: Connect with other Adobe users, ask questions, and share your expertise. The Adobe Community is a space where designers come together to discuss tools, techniques, and creative solutions.

3. Design Blogs and Magazines

Smashing Magazine: Explore a wealth of design articles, tutorials, and resources that cover various aspects of web and graphic design. Smashing Magazine is a treasure trove for design insights.

Creative Bloq: Delve into design news, trends, and tutorials on Creative Bloq. The platform covers a wide range of design topics, from UI/UX to illustration.

A List Apart: Discover articles on web design, development, and user experience. A List Apart offers in-depth insights into the intricacies of designing for the digital realm.

4. Inspirational Platforms

Pinterest: Immerse yourself in a world of design inspiration. Pinterest is a visual playground where you can discover a plethora of creative ideas and trends.

Awwwards: Explore a collection of exceptional websites and digital experiences. Awwwards showcases innovative design and recognizes excellence in web design.

Designspiration: Get your daily dose of design inspiration from Designspiration's curated collection of visuals. Discover new techniques, styles, and artistic approaches.

5. Books and Ebooks

"Thinking with Type" by Ellen Lupton: Dive into the world of typography with this insightful book that explores the principles and practices of effective type design.

"The Elements of Graphic Design" by Alex W. White: Delve into the foundational elements of graphic design, including composition, color, and typography, through this comprehensive guide.

"Steal Like an Artist" by Austin Kleon: Embrace creativity and inspiration with this book, which encourages you to draw from a diverse range of influences to fuel your own artistic journey.

In Conclusion: Nurturing Your Creative Fire

The journey of design brilliance is one of perpetual learning, exploration, and growth. With these resources at your fingertips, you have the means to elevate your craft, refine your techniques, and embrace the ever-changing landscape of design. From online courses that deepen your expertise to vibrant communities that foster collaboration, these resources are the compasses that guide you toward mastery.

As you continue your design odyssey, remember that the pursuit of brilliance is an ongoing adventure. Embrace curiosity, seek knowledge, and nurture your creative fire. Let these resources serve as beacons that light up your path and inspire you to push the boundaries of your creativity, transforming your designs into masterpieces that captivate and inspire.

GLOSSARY OF ADVANCED ILLUSTRATOR TERMINOLOGY

In the intricate world of advanced Adobe Illustrator usage, fluency in terminology is the key to unlocking the full potential of your designs. As you've explored the depths of Illustrator's tools, techniques, and capabilities, you've encountered a myriad of specialized terms that form the foundation of your creative process. In this glossary, we decipher the language of advanced Illustrator terminology, empowering you to navigate the complexities of design with confidence and finesse.

1. Bezier Curve

A mathematical curve used in vector graphics to create smooth and precise shapes. Illustrator's Pen Tool employs Bezier curves to craft lines and paths.

2. Clipping Mask

A technique that uses one object to mask another, revealing only the area that overlaps the masking object. Clipping masks are commonly used to create intricate designs and effects.

3. Curvature Tool

A tool that simplifies the process of creating smooth curves by allowing you to adjust the curvature of paths directly. It's particularly useful for creating organic shapes and intricate designs.

4. DPI (Dots Per Inch)

A measure of resolution used in both digital and print media. DPI indicates the number of dots or pixels per inch, influencing the quality and sharpness of images.

5. Gradient Mesh

An advanced technique that allows you to create intricate color blends within objects. Gradient meshes enable the creation of realistic shading and dimensional effects.

6. Opacity Mask

A method used to control the visibility of objects based on their opacity levels. Opacity masks are often employed to create subtle transitions and effects.

7. Pathfinder

A panel containing tools that enable you to combine, divide, and manipulate paths and shapes. Pathfinder tools facilitate complex shape interactions.

8. Rasterize

The process of converting vector elements into raster images, where each pixel is assigned a color value. Rasterization is necessary when exporting vector graphics for specific purposes.

9. Smart Guides

Interactive guides that aid in precise alignment and distribution of objects. Smart Guides snap to key points, enabling accurate arrangement and spacing.

10. SVG (Scalable Vector Graphics)

A format used for vector graphics that's compatible with web browsers. SVG files are resolution-independent and can be scaled without loss of quality.

11. Typography
The art and technique of arranging type to make written language readable and visually appealing. Illustrator offers advanced typography tools for creative text design.

12. Vector Graphics
Graphics composed of geometric shapes and paths defined by mathematical equations. Vector graphics are infinitely scalable without loss of quality.

13. Warped Text
A feature that enables you to bend, twist, and distort text along a specified path. Warped text adds a dynamic and artistic element to designs.

14. X and Y Coordinates
The Cartesian coordinates used to position objects in Illustrator. The X coordinate determines the horizontal position, while the Y coordinate determines the vertical position.

15. Zigzag Effect
An Illustrator effect that creates a jagged, zigzag pattern along a path. The Zigzag Effect adds texture and dynamic movement to designs.

In Conclusion: Fluent in the Language of Design Brilliance

As you navigate the complexities of advanced Illustrator usage, the mastery of terminology is your compass. Each term in this glossary unlocks a new realm of design possibilities, enabling you to communicate, create, and innovate with precision. Embrace these terms as the building blocks of your design fluency, and let your designs resonate with the depth and clarity that comes from understanding the language of design brilliance.

www.ingramcontent.com/pod-product-compliance
Lightning Source LLC
Chambersburg PA
CBHW071251050326
40690CB00011B/2342

* 9 7 9 8 8 5 6 9 0 3 1 9 4 *